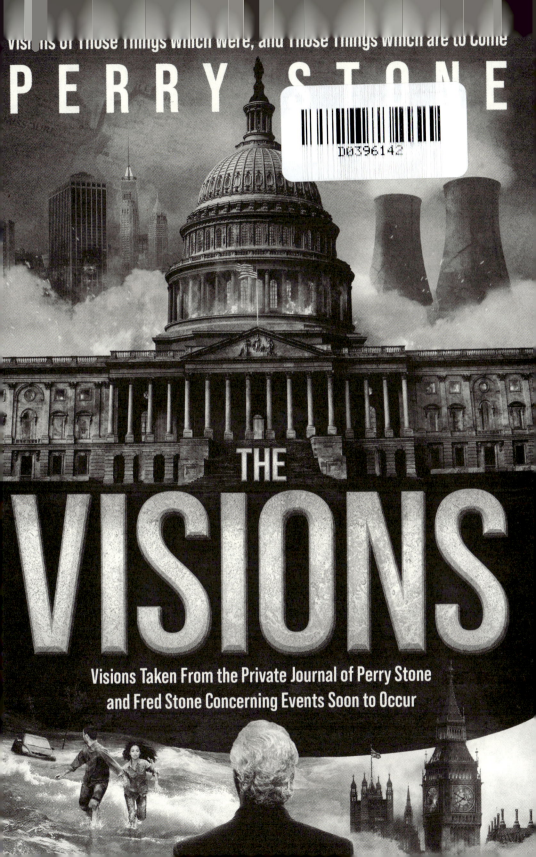

Visions of Those Things Which Were, and Those Things Which are to Come

PERRY STONE

THE
VISIONS

Visions Taken From the Private Journal of Perry Stone
and Fred Stone Concerning Events Soon to Occur

THE
VISIONS

THE VISIONS

Published by Voice of Evangelism Ministries
P. O. Box 3595
Cleveland TN 37320
423.478.3456
www.perrystone.org

Unmarked Scripture quotations are from the King James Version of the Bible.

Scripture quotations marked NKJV are from the New Kings James Version of the Bible. Copyright © 1979, 1980, 1982 by Thomas Nelson, Inc., publishers. Used by permission.

First Edition © 2022

Printed in the United States of America

ISBN: 978-0-9895618-0-8

Cover Design & Layout: Michael Dutton

CONTENTS

INTRODUCTION

Since 1977, I have personally written over one-hundred books that cover a wide range of topics, many of which focus on prophetic insights. These books explore numerous prophecies that are penned in the Bible, many of which have come to pass in our generation. Others, such as the Apocalypse (Revelation), are set to be fulfilled in the future. Throughout my nearly five decades of ministry, when engaging in long weeks of intense study, research, and information documentation, I sometimes sense a strong inspiration to turn notes into a book, and thereby allow more people to learn valuable insight.

This book carries a *different* type of insight. It contains various revelations that came to me over many years. They include past, present, and future insights received through a series of visions, including night visions while in deep sleep and open visions with my eyes closed in prayer. It is a book I have resisted writing for a couple of reasons.

First, it is easy for me to write about the dynamic and sometimes dramatic and supernatural experiences of other believers. But I sometimes struggle when writing about my own experiences, especially to the extent that will be required in many of these chapters. Saying, "I saw or heard" presents the author's point of view, perspective, or personal experience. Although I'm not comfortable writing this way, it is necessary, as most of these visions and dreams were personal, firsthand experiences.

The second challenge is sharing content that can be disturbing or troubling, as is the case with many of these visions. Everybody loves to hear faith-building, upbeat, anointed, and inspiring messages, and it can be difficult to warn of somber future events. With it comes a burden in my soul. Such warnings also create opportunities for skeptics and critics to slap labels on the subject matter, such as doom and gloom preaching, scare tactics, and a host of other accusations intended to intimidate people into silence.

But reading God's warning to the prophet Ezekiel ignites my spirit like the fire in Jeremiah's bones (Jer. 20:9) to write down the visionary experiences that have come to pass, in order to *confirm and prepare* readers for the visions that are *yet to come to pass.*

In Ezekiel 33:1-9, God tells Ezekiel that if He sends a warning to a watchman so the people will be aware of coming danger, and the watchman refuses to publicly announce the warning of God's coming judgment for national sins, God will require the blood of the people at the watchman's hand. Once the warnings are publicly released, the responsibility of obedience is transferred to the people. They have the personal choice to either repent and turn the situation around or reject the warning. If they reject the message, the hands of the watchmen and prophets are clean from blood guilt. This warning is why prophets such as Jeremiah, Ezekiel, and Isaiah refused to remain silent, even amid verbal persecution and religious opposition.

It is also important to present warnings in God's *timing.* There is a spiritual principle that God will do nothing until He first reveals His secrets to His servants the prophets (Amos 3:7). He gives them ample time to present the message before the vision manifests.

These warnings are often released publicly, in advance, giving the people to whom the warning is given time to repent, turn from their wickedness, and perhaps avoid the calamity. Such an example is Jonah warning Nineveh. The entire city repented and was spared (see the biblical book of Jonah).

Warnings that led to preparations are evident in numerous biblical narratives. Joseph warned Pharaoh of a coming seven-year famine seven years in advance. This gave the Egyptians eighty-four months to store up large portions of grain in silos before the seven-year famine struck (Gen. 41).

The righteous man Noah was moved by faith and godly fear after God warned him of a future global deluge. Noah was motivated to spend over one hundred years preparing a floating zoo and houseboat (Heb. 11:7). Ten decades of hard labor was not in vain, because when the flood waters covered the earth, Noah and his family were preserved inside the ark.

Jonah was commissioned to predict the destruction of the wicked city of Nineveh within forty days, if they did not repent. The people of Jerusalem were handed a timeframe of one generation (forty years) to prepare and escape the city before Jerusalem's utter desolation by the Roman legions (Matt. 23:36; 24:1-3).

As you read this book, pay careful attention to the first three chapters. Those present a foundational study on the history of visions and ancient oracles, along with basic biblical information to understand why and how God uses spiritual visions to bring present-day warnings and reveal mankind's prophetic future. The Bible predicts *global* impact of the tribulation judgment. However, a vision can reveal personal, family, local, or national warnings.

The book of Revelation, the last book in the New Testament, announces a blessing from God for those who read and keep the words of the book (Rev. 22:7). Joel predicted that in the last days, God would speak to His people through spiritual dreams and visions (Joel 2:28-29). We see this taking place among sons and daughters, men and women, young and old. We have entered that season. Paul wrote that we are not in darkness that this Day would overtake us as a thief (1 Thess. 5:4).

In these chapters I will set the foundation, review the past, examine the present, and unveil prophetic visions for the future. I do so in humility and with fear and trembling.

A Servant of the Kingdom,
Perry Stone, Jr.

SETTING
THE
FOUNDATION

CHAPTER 1

HEAVEN HAS BEEN WARNING THE EARTH

Moses, Ezekiel, Isaiah, John—and the biblical list goes on—had one important thing in common. God unveiled revelation to each of them, and it was recorded for the benefit of generations to come.

God gave Moses a face-to-face revelation found in the first five books of the Bible (the Torah) during his forty days on Mount Sinai.

The prophet Ezekiel pierced the veil of the upper world and saw four cherub angels bearing the throne of the Almighty, creating a *merkava,* which in Hebrew alludes to God's throne becoming a fast-moving chariot (Ezek. 1).

Isaiah, the Hebrew seer, had his spiritual eyes opened to view seraphim, a unique type of angel with six wings (Isa. 6:1-2).

In John's apocalyptic visions, he was carried by the Spirit into the throne room, where he saw living creatures and heavenly realities that were unseen by previous prophets and seers (Rev. 5).

The upper world — the heavenly dwelling place of God, Christ, and the angels — has been in contact with the lower world – the earthly dwelling place of humans – since the time of the Garden of Eden. Heaven speaks continually if anyone on earth is in tune to the frequency of the Holy Spirit and is willing to become a receptor to a divine visitation.

The Apostle Paul made three noted statements. He wrote in 1 Corinthians 13:12, "We see through a glass darkly...." The word *glass* here is a reference to polished metals used in Roman times that people would gaze into to see a reflection of their faces. Mirrors as we have today did not exist. The polished brass could give a general reflection, but the image was never completely clear. Paul also noted that, when the Almighty sent His divine messages from the celestial world to earth through His spiritual gifts (1 Cor. 12:1-3), we on earth would "know in part and prophesy in part" (1 Cor. 13:9).

The phrase *"in part"* alludes to imperfection. The Holy Bible is perfect (James 1:25). However, information received outside of the scriptures, such as discovering the will of God for our life, the plans we believe He is giving us, or advance warnings of what is coming, can be veiled in the symbolism of dreams and visions, thus requiring interpretation.

Through reading, research, and prayer, we gain knowledge. However, revelation knowledge of the unseen and unknown must be received and searched out using Scripture as our foundation. Unusual symbolism in spiritual dreams or visions is found in the Bible. The heavenly realm uses numerous methods to express warnings or instruction to humanity. Let's look at four of those.

HEAVENLY MESSENGERS

From the creation of Adam until the time that mankind received the written word from God through the Torah was 2,500 years. During this time, and until the completion of the canon of Scripture, it was common for righteous men and women to receive visitations and messages from angels. After man's expulsion from Eden, cherubim and a flaming sword were placed at the east gate of the garden to prevent Adam or his descendants from accessing the tree of life (Gen. 3:24).

In the Old Testament, angels appeared to Abraham, Lot, Jacob, Moses, Balaam, Gideon's parents, Gideon, Samson's parents, and others. In the time of David, angels were active in situations that involved Jerusalem. They were tasked with executing judgments and releasing blessings.

Elisha and his servant saw with unveiled eyes the horses and chariots of fire that were sent to protect them from an invading army (2 Kings 6:17).

Many of the prophets who penned books in the Old Testament (such as Ezekiel, Isaiah, Daniel, and Zechariah) encountered angelic messengers who brought them warnings for the Jews, Jerusalem, and Israel. They were given revelations concerning future events, some to transpire hundreds or thousands of years from their day. Much of the future insight the angel Gabriel revealed to Daniel is yet to be fulfilled. Angels are heavenly messengers who continually minister from heaven to earth.

THE TORAH, THE PROPHETS, THE WORD

Approximately 1,500 years before Christ's birth, the prophet Moses received the words found in the Torah. Moses wrote of Creation, the Flood, the history of nations, and God's covenant nation. The five books conclude with Moses' death. The Bible continues with Joshua and Judges, followed by the history of Israel and the kings of Israel and Judah. The thirty-nine Old Testament books are divided into the Torah, the Historical Books, the Major and Minor Prophets, and the Wisdom books.

The New Testament has twenty-seven books with the Gospels, the Epistles (including Paul's prison letters), and the book of Revelation. These combined sixty-six books are the inspired Word of God. In our time, one of the focuses of study is Bible prophecy and its fulfillment.

The Proverbs provide us with wisdom for living. The Gospels provide instructions for serving Christ and loving others. The Epistles give guidelines for life and the operation of the church. The book of Revelation reveals the world's prophetic future. The primary method God has chosen to speak to us is through His Word.

THREE VOCAL GIFTS

Hundreds of millions of people from all nations believe in, accept, and operate in one or more gifts of the Spirit, as mentioned in 1 Corinthians 12:7-10. Three of these nine gifts are vocal gifts—prophecy, tongues, and interpretation. Growing up, I was surrounded by great men of God who operated in these gifts, including my own father. I know of many situations where one or more of these vocal gifts operated in a church service and brought conviction to someone because of their sins, or warned of danger that was ahead.

Many Christians take the theological stance that these vocal gifts have ceased or only operated in the first century to assist in the growth of the early church. I won't argue with anyone's opinion. However, I have personally seen and experienced specific spiritual manifestations that gave clear warnings of danger, for either myself or someone else, as the Holy Spirit knows the future and can reveal the blessings and the battles along a person's path. This is one of many methods that God uses. In Acts 2:1-4, on the Day of Pentecost, there was a sound from heaven. There are still sounds from heaven if we have spiritual ears to hear.

VISIONS AND DREAMS

Most of the twenty-one dreams recorded in the Bible fall under the category of *prophetic dreams* or *warnings*. For example, the wise men who visited the infant Christ, as well as Joseph, Mary's husband, were warned in a dream of danger that would befall them if they reported Christ's birth to Herod, or if Joseph remained in Bethlehem (Matt. 2:12-13, 19).

Numerous important visions are found in Scripture. The word *vision* is used seventy-three times in the English translation of the Bible. At times, a prophet would pen that he was writing a vision from God (Obadiah 1:1). Other times, such as with Daniel, the visionary prophet saw strange beasts and unusual symbolism in visions while in prayer or in a deep sleep (Dan. 2:19; 7:2; 8:1; 9:21; 10:7).

Dreams are far more common than visions. However, Joel predicted that in the last days, when the Holy Spirit would be poured out, that old men would dream dreams and young men would see visions (Joel 2:28-29). The final end-time revival is a global harvest, larger than any in history. Throughout Scripture, any time the Holy Spirit began moving heavily in Israel, there was a resurgence of prophetic activity, including visions and dreams or angelic visitations.

The subject of dreams has been explored extensively. The subject of spiritual visions has received less attention in contemporary times because visions are not as common as dreams. It is important to explore the types of biblical visions before moving on to the numerous visions of the past and present, as well as those that reveal the future.

CHAPTER 2

FOUR TYPES OF SPIRITUAL VISIONS

Scholars indicate that the scriptures were penned by forty men who were considered prophets, historians, and men of wisdom. The biblical prophets were men who spoke as they were moved by the Holy Spirit (2 Pet. 1:21). They inked their revelations on parchments while under the inspiration of God Himself (2 Tim. 3:16).

The Greek word *inspiration* refers to God breathing out and the prophet breathing in. God's words were concealed in His *breath*. The word is *ruwach* in Hebrew, translated as *breath* and *spirit*. An example of inspiration is when the wind of God blew into the Upper Room, inspiring Galileans to speak fluently in known languages (tongues) that they had never studied (Acts 2:1-7).

Writing the words of God requires inspiration. *Seeing the warnings of God requires vision.* Predicting future events often requires a visual experience to help the visionary explain in detail what is coming. Portions of the books of Daniel, Zechariah, Ezekiel, and other inspired Old Testament books were written when a prophetic visionary saw strange symbolism, recorded angelic visitations, or was carried into the future by the Holy Spirit to see what did not exist at the time but would in generations to come.

Except for several chapters in Daniel that were written in Aramaic, the Old Testament was written in the Hebrew language. The English translation uses the word *vision* when speaking of these supernatural visitations. The most common meaning of vision refers to a person's eyesight, or their ability to see in the physical realm. The second most common usage refers to plans for the future, as indicated by the often-heard phrase, "This is our vision for the future."

In Habakkuk, the prophet was instructed to write down his vision and explain that the vision was for an appointed time; that is, some point in the future:

> *"And the LORD answered me and said: 'Write the vision, and make it plain on tables, that he may run who reads it. For the vision is yet for an appointed time; but at the end it will speak, and it will not lie. Though it tarries, wait for it; because it will surely come, it will not tarry.'"*

> — HABAKKUK 2:2-3

The Hebrew word used when Habakkuk spoke of the vision is the Hebrew word *chazon*, alluding to a mental dream or divine revelation. It can also refer to the ability to imagine or mentally create a plan or idea for the future and make it a reality. However, the spiritual definition of the word from the prophetic and biblical stories has a far deeper meaning.

Three Old Testament prophets—Isaiah, Ezekiel, and Daniel—penned the word *vision* more frequently than other prophets. In the book of Isaiah, the word vision is mentioned in seven verses. The prophet Ezekiel referred thirteen times to a vision, while the word vision is mentioned twenty-two times in the twelve chapters in Daniel, more than any other Old Testament prophet. For these biblical prophets, visions were divinely inspired visual scenes that were projected into their minds, either during prayer, during a deep sleep, or when fully awake. The wide-awake visions are the most rare and unusual. One example is when the prophet Balaam saw a vision of the Most High God and fell into a trance while his eyes were open (Num. 24:16).

These visions enabled the prophet to see beyond the earthly and into the heavenly realm, a view that is impossible with our natural eyes. Many of these visions were so remarkable that they are difficult for contemporary Christians to comprehend.

When King Uzziah died, Isaiah pierced the veil into God's heavenly throne room, where he observed angelic seraphim flying above and around God's throne. Each had six wings—two that covered their eyes, two that covered their feet, and two that were used for flying (Isa. 6:1-4).

Ezekiel's spiritual eyes were opened and he saw a fiery whirlwind forming from the north. Within the burning twister, Ezekiel described God's throne being lifted and carried on the shoulders of four angelic cherubim (Ezek. 1:1-28).

On several occasions, Daniel was visited by the angel Gabriel. In dreams and night visions, God's prophet in Babylon saw strange symbolism in the form of wild beasts that represented prophetic empires that would rise on earth (Dan. 7 and 8).

The book of Daniel is the only major book in the Bible where two languages are used—Hebrew and Aramaic. There are four different words and meanings for the types of visions that Daniel experienced. According to the *Dake Annotated Reference Bible*, the words found in Daniel are as follows:

1. The word *chazon*

This Hebrew word refers to a *mental sight, dream, revelation,* or *oracle*. It is found in Daniel 1:17, where the verse states that Daniel, "had understanding in all visions and dreams." The word is found in Daniel 8:1-2, 13, 15, 17, 26, and other references. The word can also be used when referring to a dream (Isa. 29:7) or an inspired writing (Isa. 1:1).

2. The word *chezev*

This Aramaic word simply means *sight* or *vision*. The word is found in Daniel 2:19 when Daniel received a secret from the Lord. The secret was a strange dream that the king forgot, but it was given to Daniel in a night dream from the Lord. Daniel later stood before the king and revealed to him both the dream and the interpretation. This was the famous dream of the metallic image that revealed the prophetic rise of world empires that would impact the Jews, Jerusalem, and Israel.

3. The word *mar'ah*

This word is used to describe a vision that is as though *seeing a reflection in a mirror*. The word is found in Daniel 10:7-8, where Daniel was beside the river Hiddekel in Babylon, when suddenly he was over-taken with a physical shaking that brought him on his face to the ground. He then saw what theologians identify as a theophany, which is the visible appearance of either God or Christ in the Old Testament. The man that Daniel saw in this vision was clothed in linen and wore a golden belt. His eyes were like torches of fire, his arms and his feet were like burnished bronze, and his words were like the voice of a multitude. This description is similar to the vision the Apostle John had of Christ, as recorded in the first chapter of Revelation.

4. The word *mar'eh*

The fourth word for vision, *mar'eh*, means *sight* (what is seen with the eye) or *appearance*. This Hebrew word is found in Daniel 10:1, where Daniel saw a stunning vision but did not receive the under-standing. So, he fasted for three whole weeks. Eventually, he penetrated the upper atmosphere where a strong demonic prince spirit, identified by Gabriel as "the prince of the kingdom of Persia," had formed a barrier in the second heaven that prevented Gabriel from reaching Daniel. The prophet Daniel saw the angelic visitor and heard him speak audibly. Daniel chapters 11 and 12 explain what Gabriel revealed to Daniel (Daniel 10:1-12).

POSITIONED NEAR WATER

These four words reveal that there are different types of visions and methods of receiving them. It is also interesting to note the number of times the prophet or apostle was near *water* when the vision occurred:

1. The Jewish exiles were meditating and praying beside the rivers in Babylon when they spoke under divine inspiration (Psa. 137:1).

2. Eight times, Ezekiel mentioned his geographical location as being beside the River Chebar when he tapped into the visions of heaven. For instance, he was among the captives by the River Chebar when the heavens were opened and he saw the visions of God (Ezek. 1:1). Ezekiel later stated that he was by the River Chebar when the "hand of the Lord was upon him" (Ezek. 1:3). In this opening vision, the prophet gave the most detailed description of heavenly cherubim of any prophet in Scripture.

3. The Apostle John was on the island of Patmos surrounded by the Aegean Sea when he found himself "in the Spirit on the Lord's Day" (Rev. 1:10).

4. When Daniel experienced his remarkable vision of future prophetic empires, he reported, "I was at Shushan

in the palace, which is in the province of Elam; and I saw in a vision, and I was by the river of Ulai" (Dan. 8:2).

In Scripture, water is an important symbol for the Holy Spirit (John 7:38-39). In Heaven, the floor of God's throne room is described by John as a sea of glass, like crystal, that reflects the light emitting from the glory of God (Rev. 4:6; 15:2). There is a river of water of life, clear as crystal that proceeds from the throne of God. On either side is the tree of life, bearing twelve types of fruit each month (Rev. 22:2).

There is something unique about being near a body of water. It is peaceful and calms the spirit and soul. Perhaps this is why rivers are linked with the many visions by biblical prophets. We have a pool with mountain stone in our backyard. One of my favorite times is sitting on our back porch when it is raining and listening to the rain hit the water and stone. I find it very easy to pray and meditate upon the Word as the sound and scene create a comforting atmosphere.

OPEN VISIONS

Ezekiel was a Jewish political prisoner in Babylon, by the River Chebar, when suddenly the heavens opened and he saw visions of God. The prophet described the moment as the hand of the Lord being upon him (Ezek. 1:3). The seer then detailed the appearance of cherubim lifting God's throne and traveling like lightning, with the imagery of a "wheel within a wheel" (Ezek. 1:1-28).

This vision is called an *open vision* since it occurs when the visionary is awake, fully alert, and completely aware of his surroundings. Most scholars would agree that this is the highest form of supernatural revelation. True biblical prophets lived on a high dimension of holiness and sanctity that enabled them to move from the common physical realm to immediately being carried away in the Spirit to another dimension where they connected with activities in the third heaven (2 Cor. 12: 2), the location of God's throne room.

John was on a rocky island surrounded by the waters of the Aegean Sea when suddenly he heard a voice saying, "Come up here, and I will show you things which must take place after this" (Rev. 4:1). Immediately, he was standing on the crystal floor before God's throne (Rev. 4:1-2). John reported seeing into three worlds: he observed activity in Heaven, events on Earth, and strange creatures under the earth.

Engaging in three distinct dimensions at once would be physically impossible. However, in a vision, a person can spiritually go from one location or scene to another. Ezekiel indicated that he was picked up and carried by the Spirit of God from one location to another (Ezek. 8:3). The same thing happened to Peter in Acts 8:39 when the Spirit of the Lord caught him away.

VISIONS WHILE SLEEPING

Another level of visionary experience occurs when the person is in deep sleep and receives a full color, three-dimensional vision. Here is Daniel's report of such an event:

> *"In the first year of Belshazzar king of Babylon, Daniel had a dream and visions of his head while on his bed. Then he wrote down the dream, telling the main facts. Daniel spoke, saying, 'I saw in my vision by night, and behold, the four winds of heaven were stirring up the Great Sea. And four great beasts came up from the sea, each different from the other.'"*

> – DANIEL 7:1-3 (NKJV)

Dreams have a close connection to visions while sleeping, and at times it may be difficult to separate the two. Daniel's revelations of the four beast empires occurred while the prophet was *asleep,* but it was not a dream. Daniel spoke of his *vision by night,* or *a night vision.* Every person has natural ears and spiritual ears. When sleeping, your natural ears cut off the sounds around you, yet your spiritual ears remain open, as alluded to in Job:

> *"Now a word was secretly brought to me, and my ear received a whisper of it.*
>
> *In disquieting thoughts from the visions of the night when deep sleep falls on men..."*
>
> – JOB 4:12-13 (NKJV)

> *"In a dream, in a vision of the night, when deep sleep falls upon men, while slumbering on their beds; Then he opens the ears of men, and seals their instruction, in order to turn man from his deed, and conceal pride from man."*
>
> – JOB 33:15-17 (NKJV)

The same is true with our eyes. We view our surroundings, and the visual image transfers to our brain, which translates words, colors, and sounds for our understanding. When we sleep, our natural eyes are closed, yet we see images in dreams. In those dreams we can see, hear, touch, and sometimes feel and smell. How is this possible? Because our spirit has eyes that see, just as our natural body has eyes that see. When we die and our spirit leaves our body (2 Cor. 5:8), we still retain our five senses outside of our physical body (Luke 16:19-31). Since the ears and eyes of our spirit never sleep, they are able to receive spiritual information from God, even at night while the body is sleeping.

VISIONS WHILE AWAKE

Another type of vision is the release of spiritual insight that enters the mind while a person is completely *awake*. There are different types of visions while awake, and a person might not always recognize when some of these occur.

Everyone spends time daydreaming, especially when they are young. Sometimes the child becomes present in body but absent in mind. They sit behind a desk at school, while at the same time they are mentally back home in the yard splashing in their plastic pool. *This is not a vision, but simply the imagination.* The human mind creates *images* (the root word for imagination). With a simple change in thinking, the imagination can take you any place in the world, all without paying a dime.

Then there is the Spirit-filled believer who can meditate upon the Lord and pray while sitting at a desk, walking down a sidewalk, or lying in a bed. Suddenly they may sense a strong, gut feeling that something is wrong. The weight and pressure they feel creates a *burden* in their spirit. These burdens must be followed up with intercessory prayer. Deep intercession can *reveal* what has been *concealed*, giving you previously unknown understanding, including warnings from God. This burden or revelation can also be accompanied by a sudden vision in your spirit of whatever is causing the burden.

In the New Testament, Paul wrote of *speaking by revelation* (Gal. 2:2; Eph. 3:3). The Greek word revelation in the New Testament is *apokalupsis*, which means *"to unveil, to disclose, to reveal something concealed."* In the biblical context, revelation is when the Holy Spirit opens the eyes of your understanding to something concealed from you, or something that you previously did not see or understand. A revelation is a sudden understanding of a truth or insight of which you previously were unaware.

Imagination alone can be an unproductive use of energy. However, a divine revelation can change your situation. Imagination can visually create the unseen, while divine revelation can change the seen! Visions from God are about seeing in the present to impact the future. A literal, supernatural vision is a deep manifestation that impacts the body, soul, and spirit.

Balaam was an Old Testament prophet who eventually compromised and ruined his reputation and his name in Scripture. During one encounter, he had an extraordinary experience:

> *"He hath said, which heard the words of God, which saw the vision of the Almighty, falling into a trance, but having his eyes open."*
>
> – NUMBERS 24:4 (KJV)

The phrase "having his eyes opened" can be interpreted two ways. It could mean that he was fully awake and alert with his physical eyes open, and suddenly went into a spiritual state (trance) and saw into the spirit realm. Or it could mean that his *spiritual eyes* were opened, making the invisible realm visible.

Shortly after Christ was resurrected, He met two of His own disciples on the road to Emmaus. While walking together, Christ expounded upon the prophecies of Moses (from the Torah) and other Old Testament prophecies concerning Himself. All the while the disciples were unaware of who Christ was.

In Luke 24:16, we read that "their eyes were holden," meaning that their natural eyes were restrained from seeing who He was. Suddenly, their eyes were opened (Luke 24:31). The Greek word for opened is not the common word used throughout much of the New Testament. The common word is *anoigo*, meaning "to open." This word is *dianoigo*, and it means "to open thoroughly." It alludes to seeing all the details. Spiritually it refers to having full or expounded understanding.

A *trance*, such as Balaam experienced, is a different kind of spiritual experience. Both Peter (Acts 10:10) and the Apostle Paul (Acts 22:17) speak of being in a trance during prayer. The Greek word used is *ekstasis*, from where we derive the English word ecstasy. It can mean bewilderment or astonishment, and it can even refer to being out of one's mind. Both saw something, not in their mind, but from the realm of the Spirit. Before John penned the visions he saw in the Apocalypse, he wrote, "I was in the Spirit on the Lord's Day" (Rev. 1:10). One scholar interpreted it this way: I was in the mind of God on the Lord's Day.

A few times I have experienced a trance-like state. I knew I was seeing a vision, yet at the same time I was fully aware of my surroundings and my body. In a trance, you are aware of two worlds at once: the earthly and the heavenly, or the natural and the supernatural.

Moses recorded that Balaam also experienced another strange vision involving an angel:

> *"Then the Lord opened the eyes of Balaam, and he saw the angel of the Lord, standing in the way, and his sword drawn in his hand: and he bowed down his head, and fell flat on his face."*
>
> – NUMBERS 22:31 (KJV)

Angels are supernatural spirit beings that are invisible to natural human eyes. The angel must either take on the form of a man to be seen (Gen. 19), or the covering on the natural eyes must be removed, thus allowing the individual to see what others cannot see. Only when Balaam's eyes were opened could he see the angel of the Lord blocking his path in an attempt to restrain Balaam from abusing his prophetic gift.

Oddly, Balaam's donkey saw the angel before the prophet did (Num. 22:25-33). This incident could indicate that animals have an ability to sense other world activity, such as the presence of angels or demons. I have seen dogs suddenly become agitated and begin to bark in a room when nobody was there, but I could sense a negative presence. I have also seen them lying down, looking up and wagging their tails when nobody was in the room.

God permits spiritual scales to be formed over our eyes, thus disabling our natural sense of sight and keeping us from seeing the world of angels and demons. It is rare for the scales to be removed to allow a person to see into that realm. Daniel, for example, saw a vision of God's angel (Gabriel). The men near Daniel saw nothing; but they could feel the divine presence, and they trembled and fled to hide themselves (Dan. 10:7).

Perhaps one reason God does this is to prevent fear from overtaking us. In Scripture, when prophets were permitted to see an angel of the Lord, the angel told them to *fear not*. When Gabriel appeared to Daniel, the angel's first words were, "Fear not, Daniel" (Dan. 10:12).

SOMETHING NEW BEGAN TO HAPPEN IN 2021

My father, Fred Stone, was a godly, praying man who was used mightily in the realm of spiritual gifts. I knew him to pray at least one hour a day. On numerous occasions after prayer, he would tell me that he saw something in the Spirit while he was praying.

During my nearly five decades of ministry, I have been able to sense inspiration, illumination, or revelation when praying, but seldom do I *see* something in the form of a vision. In retrospect, I believe that many times my mind was too bogged down with ministry activities to slow down, be still, and see in the Spirit. Sometimes while praying I would have my mind on other things, including numerous cares of life and my duties of the day. *A vision cannot manifest through a cluttered mind or spiritually closed ears.*

After releasing numerous cares of the ministry, it was in the spring of 2021 that I began to encounter an experience that had never occurred before. It reminded me of the narrative in which the Syrian army was planning to invade Israel. As the Syrian general plotted in secret, Elisha went into his prayer closet and began to see visions that exposed the secret strategies of Israel's Syrian enemies. Elisha's revelations were reported to the king of Israel. Instead of the Israeli army falling into the enemy's trap, the army escaped (2 Kings 6).

During the spring of 2021, I became aware that a few individuals were speaking negatively of me, and some were doing so through texts and messaging apps. I would be lying in bed at night, awake but with my eyes closed, when suddenly in full color, I would see the person's phone and could read the messages they were sending to another person. At first, it would appear blurred, but as I focused on the phone the text became clear. I also knew the names of the persons involved. I would laugh to myself as I was reading their comments, thinking, "These people have no clue that the Lord knows every thought and word they are saying and is letting me see it!" At one point, there were three men on a group message criticizing a man in a neighboring city, and one mentioned that he has a contact at the newspaper and could expose this man they didn't like.

For me, this was a new type of vision that began occurring off and on for several months before going to sleep. At times, it occurred during the day when I was praying.

In August of 2021, during a time of prayer, I saw a full color vision that shook me. A few days later, a second follow-up vision took place when flying on the ministry plane with two ministry team members, Charlie Ellis and Larry Fister. I write about these visions under the chapter *Cremation Ovens.*

THE DIFFERENCE BETWEEN VISIONS AND DREAMS

Everybody dreams, but few people ever experience a vision. A dream is more two dimensional, similar to watching a movie on a screen. A vision is a three-dimensional, full color event, often with all five senses involved. A vision is a higher level of revelation than a dream, although both are noted in Scripture to carry important messages of instruction, encouragement, warnings, or prophetic information.

According to Acts 2:16-17, in the last days when the Holy is poured out on all flesh, old men shall dream dreams, and young men shall see visions. Some have interpreted this to mean that old men dream about the *past* and young men visualize the *future*. This is a contemporary interpretation and not the meaning of the verse. There is nothing supernatural about living in the past or looking forward to the future. However, there are dreams with meanings and visions with spiritual revelations and insight.

When Joel said, "Old men shall dream dreams, and young men shall see visions" (Joel 2:28), why was it not reversed to read, "Old men shall see visions, and young men dream dreams"? In my opinion, young people need a vision that is so dramatic and clear, it becomes impossible for the individual to doubt it was from the Lord. An older person is more mature and experienced. Time and age have fine-tuned the older person's spirit to enable a quick determination about whether the dream was or was not from the Lord. The young often need a *sign* to help them believe, whereas the old can *believe* without a sign.

Today, as throughout the Bible, when the Holy Spirit becomes involved in a person's life, there are often manifestations of dreams and visions. Moses wrote, "If there be a prophet among you, I the Lord will make myself known unto him in a vision, and will speak unto him in a dream" (Num. 12:6). This verse was penned before the full revelation of the Word of God was compiled for mankind.

King Nebuchadnezzar noted that Daniel's ability to see visions and interpret dreams was because of the "spirit of the holy gods" dwelling in him (Dan. 4:8). After Joseph interpreted Pharaoh's double dream, this ruler of Egypt boasted about Joseph in Genesis 41:38, saying, "Can we find such a one as this is, a man in whom the Spirit of God is?"

The Spirit of God is always moving, as indicated by the second verse of the Bible: "And the Spirit of God moved upon the face of the waters" (Gen. 1:2). His movement is always connected with the present and future. Christ said that the Spirit will show you things to come (John 16:13). He can reveal present insights and future events long before they occur.

Here are some ways to tell the difference between a spiritual dream and a vision:

A Spiritual Dream	A Spiritual Vision
Occurs when sleeping	Can occur when asleep or when awake
Is usually like watching a movie picture	Is visually in full color and all 5 senses are alert
The images will fade quickly after waking up	Visual details remain clear for a long time
Often conceals biblical symbolism	Often conceals biblical symbolism

Here is a summary of the different types of *visions*:

- Open visions when you see with clarity and receive a revelation from God giving you warnings or instructions;

- Visions when you are asleep, and you experience a full color vision involving all five senses;

- Visions when you are awake, and the mind begins to see various images or activities;

- Visions when you are awake, and you go into a trance and see clear images.

WHY SOME SEE VISIONS AND OTHERS DO NOT

Visions do not occur daily or even weekly. I may go for weeks or months without a visionary experience. Someone asked why some individuals have these types of experiences, while others may never experience even one in their lifetime. There are three likely explanations.

1. God, by His sovereign will, can place various types of spiritual gifts within each of us.

Among the patriarchs, the Lord appeared to Abraham in a vision (Gen. 15:1). There is no biblical reference to Abraham's son Isaac receiving either a vision or a dream. However, Isaac's son Jacob was a dreamer who saw angels on a ladder that reached to heaven (Gen. 28:12). Jacob was visited by angels in a dream, and they gave him a revelation to return home to Canaan (Gen. 31:11-13). Jacob was blessed with twelve sons. Of the twelve, only Joseph appeared to have the gift of prophetic dreaming and dream interpretation. God used this young man's spiritual gift of dream interpretation, which became the key to Pharaoh releasing him from prison and exalting him to second in charge in the Egyptian administration (Gen. 40-41).

My dad experienced visions and dreams throughout his life. The majority were warnings for family members or church members, and a few were linked to national calamities. This same gift was passed on to me and my brother Phillip. We both, at times, have experienced dreams that later came to pass. Thus, for some, the ability to see and interpret visions or dreams can be a gift given by God.

2. Some Christians spend much time in prayer and intercession, making them sensitive to the Spirit.

Most people I have met who are true prayer warriors have fine-tuned their spirit to be sensitive to the Spirit of the Lord. A prime example is Daniel.

Although captive in Babylon, this young Hebrew was chosen by Nebuchadnezzar, king of Babylon, to live in the palace and serve as a representative between the government of Babylon and tens of thousands of Jewish captives. He and his three companions sat at the king's table as part of the Babylonian inner circle. We read that, despite laws forbidding prayer, each day Daniel opened his window toward Jerusalem and prayed three times a day (Dan. 6:10). That was his daily routine for over seventy years while he dwelt in Babylon. Prayer fine-tuned Daniel's mind and spirit to act as a spiritual receiver through visions and dreams, and to interpret the dreams of kings.

In Acts chapter 10, Peter was praying in Joppa while prayers and sacrifices were offered up by the priest at the temple in Jerusalem. The custom was for the priests to burn incense on the golden altar twice a day, in the morning and evening. The incense, consisting of eleven different spices, represented a sacrifice of prayers that ascended upward to God from Jerusalem (Psa. 141:2).

During prayer time, Peter experienced a strange vision while in a trance (Acts 10:10). In the vision, Peter saw a sheet carrying unclean animals. The symbolism was a revelation of how God was going to allow the Gentiles (whom the Jews considered unclean) to be converted and permitted to enter the new covenant through Christ. *Please note that the vision came while Peter was praying.*

Prayer is more than carefully selected words, originating from the mind and leaving through the mouth. True prayer from the heart is a spiritual act that opens the invisible gate of the human spirit, which then allows the Holy Spirit to pour knowledge, understanding, wisdom, or inspiration into that person. My own father was an example. When he prayed, it seemed that he could at any moment hear the voice of the Lord and respond accordingly. *Those who spend time in daily prayer are more apt to experience spiritual dreams and visions.*

3. God calls and chooses certain people from their mother's womb for specific spiritual tasks for their generation.

Paul alluded to this in Galatians 1:15 when he said that God "separated me from my mother's womb, and called me by his grace." Jeremiah was told that, before God formed him in the womb, God ordained him to be a prophet (Jer. 1:7). Jeremiah was rejected by his own people, mocked, and confined to a muddy prison. His discouragement caused him to want to quit and say nothing. However, being *chosen* by God, he could not stop warning the people, and he described it as a burning fire shut up in his bones (Jer. 20:9).

IS IT FROM THE LORD?

The Bible contains symbolism. If biblically literate Christians are asked what a serpent represents in the scriptures, they will respond, "Satan," which would be correct. If asked what a lamb represents in the Bible, they will answer "Christ," as He is called the Lamb of God that takes away the sin of the world (John 1:29). Bible students know that sheep are followers of Christ, while goats are hypocrites, doubters, or hinderers whom God will separate at the time of the end (Matt. 25:32-33).

Dreams and visions continue to be two methods by which God can speak, warn, or instruct His people. Not every dream has a spiritual interpretation; however, that is not the case with visions. When I have experienced a vision, it often contains biblical symbolism; therefore, the Bible is needed to interpret the meaning.

A dream may impact the mind, but a vision will impact the spirit. A vision will remain with you long after a dream has faded faster than a morning fog. A spiritual warning from the Lord is often followed by a great burden, which feels like a weight pressing in your soul. This spiritual pressure pulls you into your prayer closet of intercession.

A warning message from God in a dream or vision will affect your mind and spirit. Look at the reactions of King Nebuchadnezzar and Daniel when they had a dream or vision encounter. Their reaction is recorded in the following chapters and verses in the book of Daniel.

- The king's dream (2:1) — His spirit was troubled, and sleep left him

- The king's dream (2:3) — I have had a dream and my spirit is anxious to know the dream

- The king's dream (4:5) — It made me afraid, and the visions troubled me

- Daniel's dream (7:15) — I was grieved in my spirit, and the visions troubled me

- Daniel's dream (7:28) — My thoughts troubled me, and my countenance changed

- Daniel's vision (8:27) — I fainted and was sick certain days; I was astonished at the vision

- Daniel's vision (10:2, 8) — I was mourning three full weeks and had no strength

If a dream or vision is a message from the Lord, what you see and hear *will remain with you for a long time*. If it is a warning, your spirit and mind will be restless or troubled, as illustrated with Nebuchadnezzar and Daniel.

THE IMPORTANCE OF VISION

Our lives require vision, both natural and spiritual, to bring about the dreams and desires in our hearts. To build anything, whether it's a home, an office, a business, or a marriage, demands that the participants have some form of vision. The most magnificent buildings on earth began with a mental image in someone's mind. The vision is transferred from the image in the mind to a blueprint on paper, followed by a team of individuals prepared to take the written design and create a visible, three-dimensional object.

A visionary is someone who can see visions of the future, either prophetic or practical, and then plan for those things and follow through to the end. A visionary:

- is able to see something finished before it ever begins;

- has the ability to call those things that are not as though they already were;

- continues to believe in the vision, despite all opposition and hindrances;

- does not live in the past, but learns from past mistakes and avoids them in the future.

Disney World in Florida was completed and opened in 1971, but Walt Disney had passed away five years earlier. On opening day, it is said that a man who had assisted Walt turned to Lillian Disney and commented, "It's sad that Walt couldn't see this." She replied, "He did see it." His wife knew that Walt had seen it in detail, and the finished development was what he had seen. Walt was a business visionary.

When you receive a vision, a plan, or an inspiration from the Lord, you should immediately write it down somewhere—on paper, on your computer, on a phone app, or whatever works for you. Habakkuk understood that the fulfillment of a vision may not happen immediately, but it may be for a future appointed time. However, never give up *in the night* what God promised you *in the light*! Hold on to what you have seen and hide it in your heart, pray over it, and believe it will come to pass.

Most of my spiritual visions tend to conceal some type of warning. The same was true with my father. Some visions are personal warnings, others are instructions or warnings connected with the ministry, and the rest expose national or international future events.

The same is true throughout Scripture. Prophetic visionaries brought information for personal edification, warnings for the priests, the temple, or Jerusalem, and visions of war or destruction at the national level in Israel.

As you will discover, visions are occurring today and must be correctly interpreted. We can learn more about the purpose and operation of this spiritual manifestation by studying previous visions and their meanings, as well as revealing when and how they came to pass. A look at the past is important to understand the future.

Even throughout secular history, we find that God gave warnings to people, and sometimes they were unbelievers. We will review some of those situations in the next chapter.

CHAPTER 3

ANCIENT ORACLES AND SEERS

S omething within the hearts of all people causes them to want to know things about their future. This curiosity is not for Christians only. It is also evident in the secular world. Each day, millions of individuals read their horoscope, thinking they can determine what the stars have predestined for their day based on prognosticators interpreting some alleged star alignment. Others pay fortune tellers to read a deck of strange looking cards or interpret lines in the palm of their hand.

For years, television advertisements gave out phone numbers of so-called psychics who raked in millions of dollars, giving alleged psychic readings over a phone. People were amazed at what these psychics knew about them. Some of this "insight" was being revealed with computer programs that could access generational information by using a person's name and birthdate.

As far back as Egypt, ancient empires formed a special priesthood, which included those who were thought to be seers and magicians. Moses, during his confrontation with Pharaoh, encountered two powerful miracle counterfeiters named Jannes and Jambres. They used satanic power to imitate several miracles, such as Aaron's rod turning into a serpent. However, Aaron's rod became a serpent and swallowed the serpents of Egypt's top magicians.

When Joseph, son of Jacob, was exalted to second in command under Pharaoh, the Bible mentions the silver cup that Joseph placed in his brother's sack. After the cup was intentionally discovered, Joseph told his brother Judah in Genesis 44:15, "What is this that you have done? Don't you know that such a man as I can divine?" The Hebrew word for divine is *nachash*, which comes from a root that means *to hiss*, but generally means *to prognosticate* or *to see into the future*. Joseph's gift was his God-given ability to dream spiritual dreams and interpret difficult dream symbolism, which he did while in prison and when standing before Pharaoh (Gen. 40 - 41).

Moving forward in history, during the time of Jewish captivity in Babylon, the Babylonian kings surrounded themselves with "wise men" (Dan. 2:12-14). Daniel 2:2 lists four types of seers that were supposedly gifted in interpreting dreams or predicting the future. They were magicians, astrologers, sorcerers, and the Chaldeans.

The magicians were often empowered by demonic spirits to perform incantations and cast spells. The astrologers observed the heavens for alignments of constellations, comets, or falling stars. They used cosmic activity to make predictions on behalf of the king, including the best times to engage in warfare according to the heavenly signs. Babylonian sorcerers used incantations, blessings, or curses, and invoked prayers in the names of false gods. The Chaldeans were knowledgeable in the secret occult arts, which they used to tap into demonic power to divine information.

Don't be deceived into believing these types of occult arts are successful. When King Nebuchadnezzar experienced a prophetic dream that he could not remember, he called all four of these groups that he considered his wise men. He wanted them to seek the gods to reveal both the dream and the interpretation. The king's entire group of alleged wise men failed miserably. Only one man could reveal and interpret the mysterious dream from God, and that was Daniel, in whom was the Spirit of the living God.

The king threated his entire occult leadership after accusing them of preparing lying and corrupt words to speak before him (Dan. 2:9). The king eventually realized that all his seers were frauds who told him what he wanted to hear. He was prepared to kill everyone, including Daniel and his Jewish friends. However, when Daniel revealed the dream and the meaning, he became the *chief* of the wise men. Daniel interpreted several of the king's significant dreams (Daniel 2 and 4), and later experienced his own prophetic visions of future world empires (Daniel 7 and 8).

When Christ was born, wise men arrived to visit the infant king in a house at Bethlehem (Matt. 2:1-11). The Greek word for wise men is *magi,* referring to those who had studied ancient documents and star alignments. In this case, their point of reference was the prophecy of Balaam found in Numbers 24:17 —"There shall come a star out of Jacob (Israel)." God warned these men in a dream not to return to Jerusalem and reveal the location of the Christ child (Matt. 2:12).

Most ancient methods of predicting the future were not only strange, but ridiculous. For example, the Egyptians attempted to read the veins of a cow's liver or the position of tea grains in an empty cup, or determine the future by staring into water in a silver cup.

THE DREAMS OF KINGS

Throughout history, God has often given dreams or visions to world or national leaders. Two examples are Pharaoh's double dreams of a coming famine and the Babylonian King Nebuchadnezzar's dream of a metallic image that represented future empires (Daniel 2). Daniel also interpreted a troubling dream predicting that Nebuchadnezzar would have a mental breakdown that would force him from his throne for seven years (Daniel 4). At the time of their spiritual dreams, both men were followers of idols and did not have a covenant relationship with the true God. Both later converted to the God of Joseph and Daniel. God used prophetic dreams to seize their attention, and He used two Hebrew men, filled with the Spirit of God, to give a clear meaning of both kings' mysterious dreams. This indicates that God sovereignly gives dreams, visions, or revelations to whom He wills.

During the time of the Egyptian empire, in the days of Sesostris II (19th century BC), the priest of Heliopolis had a vision that he recorded. The words appear to be a prediction: "The ideal ruler for whose advent he longs - he brings cooling to the flames. It is said he is the shepherd of all men. There is no evil in his heart… where is he today… behold his might is not seen."

The Hebrew people were shepherds, and Egyptian leaders hated shepherds (Gen. 46:34). When Joseph requested that his estranged brothers meet with Pharaoh, he instructed them that, when asked about their occupations, they reply, "We raise cattle." That is because cattle were highly prized among the Egyptians. One of Egypt's leading deities was Apis, a false god in the form of a bull. During the interview, Joseph's brothers chose instead to reveal that they were shepherds. Perhaps Joseph was concerned about a well-known dream that a shepherd would conquer Egypt, and he feared that Pharaoh would reject his family and forbid them from moving to Egypt from Canaan.

The noted Jewish historian Josephus wrote about the famous, ancient dream that predicted a lamb would defeat Egypt:

"Pharaoh slept, and saw in his sleep a balance, and behold the whole land of Egypt stood in one scale, and a lamb in the other; and the scale in which the lamb was, outweighed that in which was the land of Egypt. Immediately Pharaoh sent and called all the chief magicians, and told them his dream. And Jannes and Jambres, who were chief of the magicians, opened their mouths and said to Pharaoh, 'A child is shortly to be born in the congregation of the Israelites whose hand shall destroy the whole land of Egypt.' Therefore Pharaoh spake to the midwives…"

"One of those sacred Scribes [said to be Jannes or Jambres in the Targum of Jonathan] who are very sagacious in foretelling future events truly, told the king, that about this time there would be a child born to the Israelites, who as he were reared, would bring Egyptian domain low, and would raise the Israelites: that he would excel all men in virtue, and obtain a glory that would be remembered though the ages…which thing was so feared by the king, that according to this man's opinion, he commanded that they should cast every male child which was born to the Israelites, into the river and destroy it…that if any parents should disobey him and venture to save their male children alive, they and their families should be destroyed."

— JOSEPHUS ANTIQUITIES; BOOK II, CHAPTER IX,

Here, Josephus explains that Pharaoh's motivation for plotting to slay all the firstborn sons was to prevent the rise of a male child who would ascend to authority, possibly taking Pharaoh's throne. Until I read Josephus' account, I never understood why Pharaoh would order Hebrew male infants to be killed, as these infants would grow up and eventually become part of the large Hebrew slave population that built treasure cities for the Egyptians (Exod. 1:11). Clearly, the Egyptian king was threatened by his dream.

It would be eighty years later that a *lamb* would defeat the entire empire of Egypt. This lamb was the Passover lamb offered and eaten in each house before the Exodus (Exod. 12). Using a hyssop plant, the lamb's blood was splashed on the left, right, and top outer post of the entrance to each home (Exod. 12:7). This blood prevented the destroying angel from killing the firstborn in the Hebrews' families. The lamb's body was roasted and eaten, bringing physical healing to the entire Hebrew nation all in one night. The following morning, they came out as one large covenant family, and not a feeble person was among them (Ps. 105:37).

When the death angel passed through, all Egyptian firstborns were killed, including the firstborn of the people, the animals, and the captives (Exod. 12:29). A lamb conquered an empire.

A VISION BEFORE MOSES' BIRTH

The Jewish historian Josephus also records that Moses' father, Amram, had a lengthy dream (vision) in which God appeared to him and exhorted him not to despair concerning the future. In the vision, God previewed Hebrew history from the time of Abraham, Ishmael, and Jacob, then informed Amram that He was with these men in all their ways. He told Amram that his child (Moses) would be concealed from danger and would deliver the Hebrew nation, and that his memory would be famous while the world lasts. The vision revealed that this child would also have a brother who would obtain a God-ordained priesthood, and his posterity would have it after him to the end of the world *(Josephus; Antiquities of the Jews, Book II, chapter IX)*.

Thus, historic narratives indicate that the birth of Moses, one of the world's great deliverers, was preceded by a unique prophetic dream.

Three years before the birth of Moses, a conjunction of Jupiter and Saturn occurred in the constellation Pisces (the fish), which was considered a heavenly sign of the Hebrew nation of Israel. Egyptian astrologers interpreted this as a sign that a great person was born among the Jews. Some rabbis suggest that this was yet another reason Pharaoh instructed midwives to kill male Hebrew children by throwing them into the Nile River (Exod. 1:22).

The crocodile was considered one of the many gods of Egypt, and slaying the Hebrew infants this way would serve as an offering to another Egyptian god. The true God of the Israelites had the final word, though. Over eighty years after Moses' birth, the Egyptian army was forcefully drowned in the salty waters of the Red Sea (Exod. 14).

JULIUS CAESAR

Julius Caesar was a Roman general who was the first Roman dictator. During this time, colonists from Capua (a city in Italy north of Naples) were constructing buildings when the workers came across ancient graves. They found numerous vessels and began searching each of them. The founder of the city of Capua had left a bronze tablet written in Greek, with a prediction that read as follows:

> *"When once the houses of Capys are brought to light, then a branch of the Julian house will be slain by the hand of one of his kindred; his death, however, will soon be avenged by terrible occurrences in Italy."*

Interestingly, Julius Caesar's wife had a troubling dream that their home fell apart, and she warned her husband not to go to the coliseum because he would be in danger. He ignored the warning. Unbeknownst to Julius, he would be assassinated. That day he was stabbed twenty-three times by a group of senators, and he died in the year 44 BC at age 55. Thus, the strange prophetic oracle written many years before came to pass.

Julius Caesar ignored his wife's warning dream. Later we will see that Pontius Pilate's wife also had a warning dream, and he heeded his wife's warning. One leader lived and another died.

ALEXANDER THE GREAT IN JERUSALEM

I learned of a stunning historical event while visiting the Temple Institute in Jerusalem, where a beautiful painting depicting the following event is on display.

There is a biblical, historical, and prophetic order of the rise and fall of empires. In the time of Daniel, the Medes and Persians overtook the Babylonian Empire. About two-hundred years later, the Greeks under the leadership of Alexander the Great overthrew the Persian armies. Alexander expanded his influence from Egypt to India by strengthening and enlarging his armies. It seemed there was no nation that could stop him.

After conquering Syria and Tyre, Alexander sent a messenger to deliver a personal letter to Jaddua, the high priest in Jerusalem, requesting provisions. Because the Persians had granted a decree for the Jews to return from Babylon, and even restored their golden treasures and permitted them to rebuild their temple, Jaddua informed the messengers that he supported Darius, the Persian King. Darius, of course, was an enemy to Alexander the Great.

When Alexander received this message, he became furious and vowed to take his soldiers to Jerusalem to kill the high priest and the people with him. Months later, Alexander's army seized the area of Gaza, giving him the opportunity to fulfill his vow, invade Jerusalem, and kill Jaddua. Word reached the high priest, and of course he and the people became afraid. Jaddua called for fasting and prayer for God's intervention in this dangerous situation.

One night, the high priest had a strange dream in which he was told not to be afraid, but to put on his priestly vestments and have everyone else wear white. They would be informed of the arrival of Alexander and his men.

Eventually word was sent that the army was approaching. The priest, wearing his eight priestly garments and all others in white, met face-to-face as Alexander was just outside of Jerusalem. When Alexander saw the people and the high priest in his garments, Alexander saluted the high priest instead of slaying him. Those in white surrounded Alexander's army.

This action puzzled Alexander's hardened troops, who questioned why the general did not fulfill his vow to slay these rebellious people. Alexander's reply is recorded by Josephus:

"I saw this very person in a dream, in this very habit, when I was in Dios, in Macedonia, who when I was considering with myself how I might obtain the dominion of Asia, exhorted me to make no delay, but bodily to pass over the sea thither, for that he would conduct my army, and would give me dominion over the Persians..."

At that moment Alexander asked to offer a sacrifice to God on the temple altar. It was then that the high priest opened the scroll of Daniel, and Josephus tells what occurred:

"And when the book of Daniel was showed him, wherein Daniel declared that one of the Greeksshould destroy the empire of the Persians, he supposed that himself was the person intended... he stopped taxes (on the Jews) until the seventh year, and gave Jews in Babylon and Media ability to make their own laws..."

— JOSEPHUS, BOOK XII; CHAPTER 1

CAESAR AUGUSTUS AND CHRIST'S BIRTH

It was common among ancient world leaders, especially around the Mediterranean, to seek advice from temple priests. Octavius, the father of Caesar Augustus, went to consult at a local oracle about the future of his son. When the libation offering of wine was poured out on the altar, the fire leaped to the roof of the temple.

The temple priest predicted that his son would achieve greatness, adding that this had only happened on one other occasion, when Alexander the Great came to the same temple to offer a sacrifice.

Caesar Augustus was the Roman Emperor at the time of Christ's birth. During this time, Rome and its citizens were enjoying world-wide celebrations commemorating the 750th year of Rome. Some believe that this expensive global celebration was one reason Caesar Augustus sent a letter throughout the empire requiring that a special tax be paid and a census be conducted in the hometown of every person. This is noted in Luke's gospel: "And there went forth a decree from Caesar Augustus, that all of the world should be taxed" (Luke 2:1).

Augustus led in the building or restoration of temples after being told he would rise to imperial power. The most famous ancient temple, or seat of oracles, was that of Apollo at Delphi, located on the slopes of Mount Parnassus above the Gulf of Corinth. A female priestess delivered the oracles, often through strange manners. She operated in a spirit of divination, translated in Greek as a "spirit of python." This is the same spirit Paul rebuked in a fortune teller, who immediately lost her power to foretell the future, thus causing confusion among those profiting from her (Acts 16:17-19).

At this oracle, Augustus asked how long his temple would last. The reply was, "Until a virgin gives birth to a child and yet remains a virgin." Augustus left, believing that his temple would endure forever based upon this impossible prediction. Strangely, around the time Christ was born of the virgin Mary (Matt. 1:23; Luke 1:27), the temple

Augustus constructed collapsed on its foundations without warning or cause.

Oddly, Augustus became known as "son of the god" through his adoption by Julius Caesar. The Romans also gave him the title "prince of peace" because there was peace during his reign.

In another attempt to discover his future, Augustus went to a temple on Palatine Hill in Rome. While seeking another oracle, a meteor suddenly lit up the dark sky over Rome. The female priestess put down her book and said to Augustus, "It is a sign of the future which is revealed to you. One world is ending, and another is beginning."

At the same time, a second oracle was given: "A child has just been born, who is the king of the future millennia, the true God of the world. He is of humble birth and of obscure race. His divinity is unrealized; when he at last makes himself known, he will be persecuted. He will work miracles; he will be accused of trafficking with evil spirits, but I see him as victor in the end over death, rising from the place where His murderers entombed him. He will reunite all nations."

Augustus is said to have reported this story to the Senate, who placed it in the Roman archives. It was said to have been read hundreds of years later by Emperor Constantine, who was responsible for an edict that lifted the persecution against Christians throughout the Roman Empire.

These types of oracles were resisted by all true Christians, and God's power through His servants often clashed with the priests and priestesses. Such was the case when Peter rebuked a Samarian sorcerer named Simon (Acts 8) and when Paul confronted the young woman who worked through a powerful spirit and brought much financial gain to those who promoted her. Just as the Egyptian magicians could, for a brief time, imitate the miracles of Moses, these oracles could predict events to occur—events that were already known in the spirit world of angels and demons, and could be made known through familiar spirits. However, when the Almighty God sent a message, only men of God with the true spirit of God could interpret it.

CHANGING THE COURSE OF HISTORY

Dreams and visions can change the course of history if their warnings are properly followed. An excellent example is recorded in Matthew 27:19.

Pontius Pilate was the procurator of the region where Christ would be legally condemned. Christ's accusers had sent Him to Pilate to stand trial in hopes that He would be condemned to death. The morning of the public trial, Pilate's wife sent word to him of a warning dream she had experienced concerning Christ:

> *"While he was sitting on the judgment seat, his wife sent to him, saying, 'Have nothing to do with that just Man, for I have suffered many things today in a dream because of Him.'"*
>
> – MATT. 27:19 (NKJV)

After receiving this warning, Pilate made every attempt to declare Jesus guiltless of any false accusations being presented against Him. Pilate declared Christ innocent. When Pilate saw that the religious Pharisees and the angry mob would not listen to him, he asked for a bowl of water. Washing his hands, he declared himself free from Christ's blood.

Who was Pilate's wife? The Gospels do not reveal her identity, but a church tradition called her Saint Procula, later Claudia Procula, and taught that she became a follower of Christ. Some go so far as to suggest (based on tradition) that the Claudia referred to in 2 Timothy 4:21 may have been the wife of Pilate. An early letter written in Latin says that she sought out Christ to heal her son Philo's crippled foot.

CONSTANTINE'S VISION

From AD 64 under Emperor Nero until the rise of Emperor Constantine the Great, Christians were greatly persecuted, tortured, and often put to death under ten Imperial Roman Emperors. This was called "the ten persecutions."

The church father Eusebius recorded that on October 28 in the year 312, a Roman civil war battle called the Battle of Milvian Bridge occurred. This battle between Constantine and Maxentius would decide which of the two would be the true emperor of Rome. On the eve of the battle, while asleep in his tent, Constantine saw an angel descend from the sky holding a glowing golden crucifix. Emblazoned in the sky were the words "conquer by this." The day of the battle, the enemy troops were on a bridge when it collapsed, drowning many of the soldiers of Maxentius.

After the battle, Constantine accredited his victory to the God of the Christians. As a result of this victory and the unusual vision, Constantine enacted the Edict of Milan in AD 313. This edict ended the state persecution of Christians, bishops, and churches.

Eusebius wrote the following after Constantine's death in the year 337: "Constantine saw with his own eyes the trophy of a cross of light in the heavens, above the sun, and bearing the inscription, CONQUER BY THIS. At this sight, he himself was struck with amazement, and his whole army also, which followed him on this expedition, and witnessed the miracle."

This dream-vision changed the course of Christianity and the Christian church, which would later become the official religion of the Roman Empire.

WHAT LACTANTIUS SAW

Lactantius was born in North Africa in AD 240 and died in AD 320. He was a respected Christian apologist and one of the most quoted and reprinted among the Latin church fathers. He began teaching under Roman Emperor Diocletian. When the emperor started persecuting Christians, Lactantius resigned and returned to the West.

His writings had a direct influence on Emperor Constantine. Lactantius wrote apologetics, including a noted treatise called *Divine Institutions*. He wrote several volumes of discourse on the Christian worldview that he addressed to pagan critics. In a section of book VII, chapter 15, he penned a discourse on Devastation of the World and Change of Empires. He began by referring to Egypt's fall and the release of Israel:

> *"Since at that time, the people of God were one, and in one nation only, Egypt, was smitten. But now, because the people of God are collected out of all languages, and dwell among the nations, and are oppressed by those bearing rule over them, it must come to pass that all nations, that is the whole world, be beaten with heavenly stripes, and the righteous people, who are the worshippers of God may be set free."*

His theory was that, since the Jews were scattered throughout the nations and were being mistreated, God was going to judge the world, which to him would have meant the nations subject to the Roman Empire. He taught that, as the end of the world approaches, human affairs must undergo a change. Righteousness would decrease, while impiety (a lack of reverence), avarice (greed for wealth), and lust would increase. Lactantius predicted that good men would become prey to the wicked and harassed on all sides by the unrighteous; that all justice would be confounded; and laws would be destroyed. There would be no security, nor government, nor any rest from evil wars that would rage everywhere. He also noted that neighboring states would carry on conflicts with other states.

THE EAST AND WEST POWERS

In his discourse, Lactantius predicted the complete fall of the Roman Empire: "The Roman name by which the world is now ruled will return to Asia: and the East will again bear rule and the West will be reduced to servitude."

Constantine placed confidence in Lactantius to the point of asking him to mentor his son. Some historians believe that the prediction of the rule of Rome being transferred to Asia and the rise of rule in the East indicated that the Western half of the Roman Empire, then centered in Rome, would decline and a new headquarters would be erected in the East. Emperor Constantine divided the Roman Empire, formed a new Eastern division in Asia Minor (today Turkey), and named the city Constantinople after himself.

The prediction proved correct, as years later, ten Germanic tribes overran the western half of the empire, eventually collapsing Imperial Rome. At the same time, the Eastern division became the center for the Christian Byzantine Empire. This empire prospered and grew. It was the Byzantines who marked the holy sites in the Holy Land and built large churches. Some ruins can be visited in Israel today. The economy grew, as indicated by the gold coins minted and placed in circulation. The Byzantine Empire continued for a thousand years, until Constantinople was overrun and captured on May 29, 1453 by Muslim armies led by Sultan Mehmed II of the Ottoman Empire.

At the fall of the Byzantine Empire, political prowess and military strength slowly moved back to the West through the British Empire. At the conclusion of World War II, the United States became the world's superpower and began a journey similar to that of Rome. Once again history changed course, as it often does when sudden events alter the course of nations.

Among the ancients, we see that world leaders, military generals, and those in high positions sought out oracles to inform them of the future. There are examples of a king's entire group being deceived and giving out the wrong information. King Ahab asked four hundred of his palace prophets whether he would win should he go to battle. All said the king would be victorious, except one man who was brought out of the king's dungeon and predicted the king's death. One man was right and four hundred were wrong!

Prior to Ahab's death, Elijah challenged 850 false prophets and prophets of the grove to a showdown at Mount Carmel. None of the prophets of the false god could produce fire. But after Elijah offered a 63-word prayer, fire fell on the altar and consumed everything on it, including the altar itself.

In Babylon, the highest-level magicians, astrologers, and wise men all failed to correctly discern and interpret the king's dreams. This is one of many reasons why, in the Torah, God forbade those in covenant with Him to seek outside sources such as soothsayers, palm readers, or those engaged in occult practices, such as witches. He knew that their methods and abilities were flawed and, at times, demonically inspired. God's revelation comes through His Word, his holy angels, and the Holy Spirit.

WARNING TO ABRAHAM LINCOLN

Moving to more contemporary times, Abraham Lincoln was America's sixteenth president. He was known as a man of great faith and prayer, and he understood Scripture. History records a warning dream that he received while serving as president:

"I retired very late. I had been up waiting for important dispatches from the front. I could not have been long in bed when I fell into a slumber, for I was weary. I soon began to dream. There seemed to be death-like stillness about me.

Then I heard subdued sobs, as if a number of people were weeping. I thought I left my bedroom and wandered downstairs. There the silence was broken by the same pitiful sobbing, but the mourners were invisible. I went from room to room; no living person was in sight, but the same mournful sounds of distress met me as I passed along. It was light in all the rooms; every object was familiar to me; but where all the people who were grieving as if their hearts would break? I was puzzled and alarmed. What could be the meaning of all of this? Determined to find the cause of a state of things so mysterious and so shocking, I kept on until I arrived at the east room, where I entered.

There I met with a sickening surprise. Before me was a catafalque, on which rested a corpse wrapped in funeral vestments. Around it were stationed soldiers who were acting as guards; and there was a throng of people, some gazing mournfully upon the corpse, whose face was covered, others weeping pitifully.

'Who is dead in the White House?' I demanded of one of the soldiers. 'The President,' was the answer. 'He was killed by an assassin!' Then came a loud burst of grief from the crowd, which awoke me from my dream. I slept no more that night and although it was only a dream, I have been strangely annoyed by it ever since."

Two weeks later, after Lincoln was assassinated by John Wilkes Booth at Ford Theatre, his casket was placed in the East Room of the White House and guarded by soldiers, just as he had seen in his dream.

Lincoln also received a vision of his death. One evening he was home and was completely exhausted. There was a mirror near him. As he looked in the mirror, he saw two faces of himself, with the tip of one nose about 3 inches from the other. One face was strong, and the other was a ghostly pale, the color of death. The vision disappeared. He wrote of it as just being tired. Later when he told his wife, she interpreted the vision to mean that he would serve two terms as president. He would be strong in the first term and die in the second term, which to her was the meaning of two faces.

The night before Lincoln went to Ford Theatre, he met with his cabinet and said several strange things, later reported to the public. He seemed troubled. He said to his men, "Gentlemen, before long you will hear some important news..." When asked what it would be, he replied, "I have heard nothing, but you will hear tomorrow." He continued, "I have had a dream three times, and again last night. I am in a boat, alone and on a boundless ocean. I have no oars, no rudder, I am helpless, and am drifting..."

On Lincoln's security team was a man named Crook. He later noted that each night, Lincoln would greet him by saying, "Good night." However, before entering the theatre, he looked at Crook and said, "Goodbye."

Clearly, Lincoln received warning dreams and a vision of what was coming. On April 14, 1865, Lincoln was shot. He died the next day.

From ancient times to the present, from the days of Abraham, Isaac, and Jacob, to the revelation of John penned in the Apocalypse, the Almighty has released mysteries concerning the future to men and women on earth. He uses dreams, visions, and visitations from angels. These types of supernatural manifestations will continue during the days leading up to the Messiah's return.

PROPHETIC DREAM GIVEN TO TWO PAGAN WORLD LEADERS

One fact that often puzzles well-informed Bible students is that, throughout Scripture, God has allowed people who have no redemptive covenant and no faith in the true God to receive significant prophetic dreams. Kings and leaders who were pagan idol worshippers received stunning warning dreams and revelations. Why would God speak to pagan leaders and reveal the future?

To understand this enigma, consider that information about future events is often known in the spirit realm—whether it is the world of angels and demons (or familiar spirits)—days, months, years, or even hundreds of years before the actual events happen in the natural realm.

Scripture gives several prime examples. Nearly seven hundred years before the birth of Christ, Isaiah wrote, "Therefore the Lord himself shall give you a sign; Behold a virgin shall conceive and bear a son, and they shall call his name Immanuel" (Isa. 7:14). This prediction was given hundreds of years in advance, and therefore it was known in the spirit world.

The same prophet Isaiah wrote of the fall of Lucifer, the name translated in the English Bible for the fallen angel Satan (Isa. 14:12). Isaiah predicted that Lucifer would be "brought down to hell, to the sides of the pit" (Isa. 14:15). The book (scroll) of Isaiah was read in the synagogue in Christ's day. We know this because Christ quoted from Isaiah 61:1-2 when He preached His first sermon in His hometown of Nazareth.

Christ cast evil spirits from the man living in a graveyard in the country of the Gadarenes. The spirit named Legion possessing the man spoke to Christ and made a strange request. He said, "Do not send us into the deep" (Luke 8:31). The Greek word for deep is *abyss*, or the pit that will become the eternal prison for Satan and his dark spirits. It seems that the demon or demons possessing this man knew the prediction of their future doom from the prophet Isaiah.

TWO PAGAN LEADERS

Some would not consider Pharaoh and King Nebuchadnezzar pagans, if the definition is "a person holding religious beliefs other than those of main world religions." In Pharaoh's day, the false gods of Egypt were considered mainstream and part of the cultural trend. The Babylonians worshipped Marduk, the chief god of the city and Babylonian empire, along with lesser gods and goddesses. To the general population, these were the ruling deities in Mesopotamia. They were worshipers and believers—but of the wrong thing. The same stones that were used to build a temple were used to form a rock with a face that was worshipped.

Despite their religious deceptions, both leaders were given amazing prophetic dreams. In the time of Joseph, the pharaoh of Egypt dreamed twice of a coming famine. Only Joseph could interpret the warning dream (Gen. 41).

Centuries later, an astonishing prophetic dream was revealed to King Nebuchadnezzar in Babylon. The king saw an image made of gold, silver, brass, and iron, with feet a mixture of iron and clay (Dan. 2). Daniel was called into the king's court to interpret the dream.

When we ponder why the true God gave spiritual dreams to these ungodly leaders, the answer is linked to the two dream interpreters. The dreams were not just for the leaders. God desired to raise up Joseph in Egypt to spare the Hebrews in time of famine. Joseph's gift of dream interpretation became the open door to Joseph's exaltation from prison to the place. The same was true with Daniel. His gift of knowledge, along with dream and vision interpretation, lifted him into the palaces of the Babylonian and Persian kings. The purpose was so that both world leaders would know there was only one true God who revealed secrets to His servants (Dan. 2:28).

THE LION'S GATE IN JERUSALEM

There are seven open gates built into the walls of the Old City of Jerusalem. Two are on the eastern side. The Golden Gate (also known by Christians as the Eastern Gate) that faces the Mount of Olives makes the eighth gate, but that is sealed with large stones. Saint Stephen's Gate, which rises above the steep bank of Jerusalem's Kidron Valley, is also called The Lion's Gate.

The Lion's Gate is important for Christian tourists because it is near the first Station of the Cross on the famous Via Dolorosa. It also is close to the biblical pool of Siloam, the place alluded to in John 5:4 where the angel troubled the water. This gate is also the entrance to the Muslim quarter of Old Jerusalem, and it is the gate closest to the Temple Mount's northern wall.

Beginning in 1517, the Ottoman Turks possessed Palestine (which was renamed Israel in 1948) and were in control of Jerusalem. They rebuilt the upper walls on Jerusalem's existing outer walls that surrounded the old city. A Turkish leader, a Muslim named Sultan Suleiman the Magnificent, was said to have had a dream in which he was devoured by a wild beast for not rebuilding the walls of Jerusalem. He immediately began the rebuilding process. When he completed the project in 1538-1539, he carved two stone lions on the outer facade of the gate to commemorate his success.

The Turks retained control of Jerusalem from 1517 to 1917, when the city transferred to the hands of the British, who held it for thirty-one years. They relinquished their control to Jordan and Israel after Israel was reestablished as a nation in 1948. The British mandate ended May 14, 1948.

Prior to June 1967, the Lion's Gate was under the control of the kingdom of Jordan, Israel's Arab neighbor. However, during the Six-Day War, Israeli paratroopers entered Jerusalem through the Lion's Gate when they retook the city.

Throughout history, there have been times when pagan leaders of significant nations and geographical prophetic regions have experienced unusual warnings or prophetic dreams. In these cases, we should not focus on the vessel that God uses; instead, we should focus on the importance of the message itself. World leaders from ancient empires loaded their inner circle with men claiming to be knowledgeable in interpreting omens. In the cases of Pharaoh and Nebuchadnezzar, their dreams and symbolism came from God and required a *true man of God,* in whom was the Spirit of God, to interpret the warnings concealed in symbolism. Their interpretations proved to be one hundred percent correct.

VISIONS
FULFILLED

CHAPTER 4

SEEING THE 9-11 ATTACK FIVE YEARS BEFORE

In June of 1996, I received one of the most significant visions I had ever experienced. I was ministering at the Assembly of God in Brooksville, Florida, pastored by David Garcia. It was a beautiful afternoon. I was eating Sunday dinner at the home where I was staying, along with Don Channel, a fellow minister who was traveling with me.

About three o'clock in the afternoon, I suddenly became overwhelmed with a feeling of extreme tiredness. I excused myself from the table to lie down in the bedroom and rest. I took my large, black leather Dake Bible and randomly opened it to read a few verses. Within minutes, I was on my right side, with my head on the top of the Bible.

I went into a sudden, deep sleep and experienced a full color vision. I found myself standing at the bottom of a paved road, looking up toward the top of a hill where this road ended at a large, solid concrete wall. On either side of the road were sidewalks and one-level red brick homes. I was walking on the left sidewalk barefooted. In dream interpretation, being barefooted would imply being unprepared for that which is ahead.

As I approached the top near the wall, I looked up into a blue sky and noticed that behind the concrete wall, looming into the atmosphere, was a solid black square cloud. Out of curiosity, I climbed on

top of the wall to see what was behind it. While standing on the wall, I saw in front of me a large field with row after row of ripened corn with beautiful green stalks. From my vantage point, looking from left to right, the corn rows seemed endless. However, directly in front of me, the cornfield ended at what appeared to be a tall structure, hundreds of yards away. The structure looked exactly like one of the World Trade Center buildings in New York City.

To my shock, the black square cloud I saw in the sky was the top part of this tall building. The building, from top to bottom, was completely shrouded in black. Positioned to the left and right side of this building were five greyish clouds, in the exact formation of tornados. Each one was as tall as this building. Suddenly the tornado on the left began to spin violently, which then triggered the one beside it to spin, leading the third, the fourth, and finally the fifth tornado to spin. Once all five were in motion, the grey tornado on the left moved from the building toward where I was standing near the wall. As it moved quickly, it began ripping up a huge swath of corn, leaving behind complete desolation. The same activity followed with each tornado taking out an entire row of corn, utterly uprooting everything in its path. In the massive field were five paths where beautiful cornstalks had been totally uprooted.

As these five grey twisters began spinning, I saw what looked like sparks of fire originating inside each of them. Each tornado spun, throwing grey dust and emitting sparks as they moved into the large cornfield. As these twisters of dust traveled in my direction (toward the wall), I felt a sense of panic and fear, causing me to jump from the wall. I turned my back from the field and ran barefooted down the left sidewalk as I attempted to make it to the bottom of the road. I was yelling, "We have to get to the cleft of the rock!" I remember yelling this twice, at the top of my lungs. When I reached the bottom of the road, I suddenly came out of the vision.

My body was literally shaking when I came out of the vision, and my mind was spinning like those clouds. I jumped up from the bed and immediately went across the hall to Don Channel's room and knocked on his door. He commented, "Man, you look like you've seen a ghost."

I told him every detail of the vision I had just experienced. We were both stunned, with no clear interpretation of the meaning. I knew this was not a normal weather disaster, but something more sinister and destructive. I knew that the building was in the same shape and height of the famous World Trade Center. I did discuss the possibility that some attack might be coming. However, I was unclear as to why the entire tower was shrouded in black, or why the upper square portion was seen in the sky before the entire building was covered in black.

That Sunday night at church I told every detail of the vision to those present. For years, including at my larger conferences, I would tell the vision. In 1999, a local Cleveland artist named J. Michael Leonard drew a series of renderings based upon what I described to him. These were shown on national television. My father and I taped a television program in which I mentioned the vision and stated that it could be a future attack on the World Trade Center. On February 26, 1993, at 12:17 PM, Islamic radicals had already attempted to bring down a Trade Center building when a bomb exploded in a basement level parking garage.

A SECOND SERIES OF VISIONS

Months later I experienced a second series of visions, all the same night, that also involved five greyish tornadoes. This time I was on a street in a large city and began hearing a chorus that sounded like a multitude of people shouting from different directions, "The storm is coming! What should we do?" I led those near me into a downtown church that was constructed from large stones (not bricks). Once inside I saw three

different ethnic groups—African Americans, Hispanics, and Asians, both men and women—all huddled together with their ethnic groups. Some were hugging each other and crying, while others were huddled together praying.

As I watched these people who looked overwhelmed with fear, I turned toward the doors of the church, which were fully opened. Seeing outside, I counted five grey tornados spinning past the church. Because these five were much closer to me, as they passed, I could see all kinds of paper, cans of soft drinks, and other objects that one would find in a business office.

When the last tornado passed, the people walked out of the church with dazed, shocked looks on their faces as they stared in disbelief. Few people said anything, but they walked like someone lost in a forest, with no real direction. Near the church, on their property, was an old cemetery. The grounds of the cemetery were covered with debris, paper, and other objects that the grey clouds had dropped.

Suddenly, the vision shifted into the downtown area. I looked around and it was evident that a major disaster of some kind had struck the city. Looking up and around, there were tall glass office buildings with windows that were cracked and some broken. In the office complex closest to me, all the offices were in total disarray, as though the storm had struck inside each office. I did not see anybody inside any of those buildings. I could see desks, filing cabinets, and office equipment that were still intact. Yet, there was chaos and confusion. Office and board room chairs were toppled and tables overturned. Some buildings nearby had survived, but others were destroyed from the inside.

After this scene, I turned to the right, where I was standing in front of a red brick shotgun style church. On the ground a few feet from me were five large, greyish pearls, each the size of a quarter, which were on a necklace that had been separated from the string that once held them together. At that moment I understood these were my personal pearls, and each was connected to the ministry. I reached down and picked

them up one-by-one, putting the pearls back on the string to reform the necklace.

I looked back to my left and saw relief workers, including firemen, assisting those who lived in the city by bringing clothes, toys for children, food, and bottled water. These were placed in piles and on pallets on the sidewalks in front of the buildings. People were picking up what they needed.

I understood the symbolism of the church, the people praying in church during a crisis, the red brick church, and relief aid being handed out. However, it was difficult at the time to paint a clear interpretation of the meaning, especially seeing the five grey tornados once again. I did believe the visions were connected in some manner.

In 1999, I shared these visions to thousands of people at our yearly Main Event meeting, which at that time was hosted in Pigeon Forge, Tennessee. I also told these visions and showed the drawings by J. Michael Leonard at a major prophetic conference. After a few years of seeing nothing happen, I placed the three drawings in a closet in my personal ministry office.

During the first week of September 2001, I was cleaning out the closet when I came across the three drawings that showed the cornfield and the blackened tower, the three ethnic groups inside the church, the outside scene of the buildings, the brick church, and the people on the sidewalks in the large city. I recall walking from my office with the pictures and showing the drawings to one of my employees. In what was later proven to be prophetic, I told him, "I think there could be an attack on the World Trade Center sometime in the future."

SEPTEMBER 11, 2001

The morning of September 11, 2001, my staff and I were at the Voice of Evangelism ministry center. It was a busy morning. Some were answering calls and the shipping department was filling orders. Suddenly, one of our receptionists rushed into the room and said, "People are calling and saying that a plane has flown into the World Trade Center!" I thought that surely it must have been a small plane, and perhaps the pilot had a heart attack. Soon another plane, a large commercial airliner, struck the second tower. By that time, media outlets were reporting that this was possibly a terrorist attack.

We had no television at the office, so I jumped in my car, drove home, and turned on the news. Every channel was reporting breaking news. The black smoke from the first airplane impact was billowing upwards, reminding me of the grey cloud around the black square in the sky that I saw in the 1996 vision. Even though I had seen the vision five years earlier, I still was shocked watching the news reports. When the buildings collapsed, the impact created a wind of spinning smoke and grey ash as it rushed through the atmosphere and down the streets. Within the grey billowing clouds were papers and debris from inside the offices of the World Trade Center.

Later I learned from a first responder that many people ran into churches, not far from ground zero. One was Trinity Church, which intersects Wall Street and Broadway in the Financial District of Lower Manhattan. Another was Saint Paul's Chapel. When I looked these up on the internet, the outside of Trinity was the same type of stone I saw in the second vision. On the grounds of Saint Paul's Chapel was an old cemetery.

Why were there five tornados? Grey tornados represent destruction the enemy is bringing. First, the two Trade Centers fell, and the tornadoes were spinning off those buildings. Five other buildings numbered Trade Center 3, 4, 5, 6 and 7 were impacted and had to be demolished. The five tornados took out five rows of corn, which is a biblical metaphor for prosperity. In the Old Testament, when grains filled the silos, it indicated spiritual and agricultural blessings. When the grain was destroyed, it was perceived as a sign of judgment. The 9-11 attacks destroyed millions of jobs, and not just in New York City. Repercussions were felt nationally and globally. Offices of large corporations were destroyed in just a couple of hours. Thousands of families were impacted by the deaths of people they loved and depended on. One of the first offices hit that day was a global financial services firm that lost 658 employees in the attack. That represented over 68% of their total New York workforce.

It should also be noted that five is the biblical number of grace, so in the midst of the storms, God gives us grace to make it through.

Why was there a wall in the first vision? This could have a dual meaning. Biblically, standing on a wall can represent being a watchman on the wall, and watchmen are required to sound a warning of events to come (Ezekiel 33). In the vision, the wall itself never collapsed, but from the wall I could see the impact of the storms coming off the black shrouded tower in the vision.

The outer boundary of the attack was not far from the eight blocks of Wall Street, which is considered the geographical center of American finance and capitalism. Symbolically, Wall Street represents the financial center of America because it is home to the Federal Reserve and the U.S. stocks, bonds, and securities markets.

The phrase *"get to the cleft of the rock"* is self-explanatory from Scripture. The psalmist used the metaphor that God is our rock, alluding to the Almighty being our stability, safety, refuge, and security, even in times of storms (Psa. 89:26; Isa. 4:6). When God delivered David from the hands of his enemies, David said, "The Lord is my rock and my fortress and my deliverer" (2 Sam. 22:2). When Moses found himself in a national crisis, he was instructed by the Lord to come into His presence, in the cleft of a rock (Exod. 33:21-22).

THE FIVE PEARLS

It is possible that the vision of restringing the five pearls could have a double reference. In Scripture, some prophetic verses can have a primary and a secondary meaning. The same can be true with prophetic dreams.

For years, I attempted to connect the five grey pearls to the five grey tornadoes. Yet, after the 9-11 attacks, there was no "break" in the ministry. In fact, more people desired to learn biblical prophetic truths than ever before. Thus, the five pearls in front of the church remained a mystery.

Christ used pearls to represent the value of the gospel and the kingdom. In Matthew 13:45-46, He said that the kingdom of heaven is like a merchant seeking beautiful pearls who finds one pearl of great price and sells all he has to buy it. Christ also instructed us not to cast our pearls before swine (Matt. 7:6), meaning, don't present sacred truth to those who mock and trample it under their feet. I perceived that the pearls represented my traveling ministry in local churches.

It is possible that this aspect of the vision was an advanced warning that my ability to travel and minister in churches would be interrupted for five months. When Covid-19 struck and began spreading in 2020, pastors canceled their special speakers and meetings. Our ministry canceled three Warrior Fests, a Prophetic Summit, and the Main Event that year; that is five events which are our most important events of the year. I came off the road for five months, eventually using social media and television programs to reach people. In the vision, at the conclusion of the storm, the five pearls were restrung, which I interpreted as the ministry continuing.

Since I previously had told this vision on Christian television, I was asked to do interviews by phone and on live Christian television on September 12 and 13 following the attacks. The FBI later released some surprising information, revealing that the terrorists posed as men who wanted to learn to fly a plane and took flight lessons at a school in Florida. They were in Florida at a location thirty minutes from where I was on that Sunday in June 1996 when God gave me the warning vision.

We later learned that other believers around the world had received warning dreams and visions from the Lord about trouble coming to New York City, and some specifically saw the World Trade Center. Thousands of people died that day, yet the lives of many were spared simply because something caused them to be late for work.

God gives warnings in advance so people will repent, and so believers will pray and be protected in the midst of the storms.

CHAPTER 5

VISION OF THE OIL RIG EXPLOSION

The following vision occurred at least two years before the fulfillment of the actual event. I told this publicly on several occasions, and I also contacted minsters in the area who might be impacted by what I had seen.

The vision, which occurred while I was in a deep sleep, began with me standing on the coast of Louisiana, looking across the Gulf of Mexico. I could see the oil rigs positioned in the Gulf. Through the years, I have traveled with minister friends and fished for sheepshead and redfish in this same area of the Gulf, so I was accustomed to seeing these large rigs rising like metal giants from the deep waters.

In the vision, I looked across the water in the distance and saw one lone oil rig. Suddenly, a large black tornado moved toward the rig and platform. It struck the rig, turning the platform into a tornado of black oil spinning over the water.

The vision then broke into several different scenes. In one scene, I was standing next to an 18-wheel tractor-trailer. One entire side panel on the trailer was missing, enabling me to look inside the container. It was empty except for one single dress displayed on a mannequin stand.

This scene changed, and I was standing at an escalator, the type you would see in a large mall that carries people from lower and upper levels. In this scene, the escalator was not moving. I saw five people, both men and woman, who appeared to be between the ages of thirty to fifty. They were lying on the ground, moaning, with their hands out and saying, "Give us money. Help us, we need money." Oddly, these five seemed to have scars on their body, but they were not real; their scars were fake. I shook my head and said, "They want help, but they actually don't need it."

In the next scene, I was transported to a seafood restaurant. The place was full of people chattering endlessly, as on any normal day. I remember briefly walking away, and when I returned, everyone was gone. Not one person was in the restaurant, including customers, cooks, servers, and managers. Looking outside the glass doors, I saw that the parking lot had no cars. I wondered what happened so fast to empty out this place.

Instantly I found myself in a different location. This time I was standing inside a small concrete building with a close minister friend,

Rusty Domingue, and a well-known local pastor, both of whom lived in Baton Rouge, Louisiana. The double doors of the building were open, revealing in the distance a small town with a main street. Every small business on the main street was closed. There was no activity at all in the town. I recalled the first part of what I saw, the spinning oil tornado. I said to myself, "This has something to do with that oil rig and the black tornado."

A few months after receiving this vision warning, I was impressed to contact a minister friend, Dino Rizzo, who at the time was pastoring Healing Place Church in Baton Rouge. I shared with him the details of the vision and suggested he prepare his church ministry outreaches, as something would eventually happen on the coast that would economically impact malls, restaurants, and small businesses.

THE RIG EXPLOSION

The vision was fulfilled on April 20, 2010, when the Deepwater Horizon oil rig, located in the Gulf of Mexico about forty-two miles off the Louisiana coast, exploded and burned, eventually capsizing into the sea. Pictures of the smoke ascending from the rig platform had the appearance of a large black tornado. Sadly, eleven workers lost their lives in the explosion.

The greatest environmental and economic impact came from what was happening *under* the water. The oil pipe, drilled deep into the oil well under the sea, was pouring black oil into the water in what became the largest marine oil spill in history. By the time the wellhead pipe was capped eighty-seven days later, an estimated three million barrels of oil had leaked into the Gulf.

THE AFTERMATH

The vision revealed the aftermath of the oil rig explosion on the economy. The oil that covered the water in the Gulf impacted the coastal waters and sea life of Louisiana, Mississippi, Alabama, and Florida. The lucrative fishing industry along the coast of Louisiana was destroyed for a long period of time. My friends from Baton Rouge informed me that many of the seafood restaurants had to close—some permanently and others for several months.

Businesses that depended on beaches and tourism were forced to operate at reduced capacity or shut their stores altogether. State and federal government agencies offered financial assistance to those in need, and churches helped as well. However, it was discovered that some people lied about needing financial assistance, just as I was shown in the vision. Each scene in this vision came to pass according to the very details in which they were seen.

In an interesting turn of events, Pastor Dino Rizzo, whom I had contacted about the vision a year prior to the rig explosion, called me in July 2010 to tell me that he had shared this vision with his staff and church. He asked me to come to the church (Healing Place) in Baton Rouge and share the details of the vision. It had been over two months since the explosion, but the crisis was continuing. I brought with me the original paper that I had written the vision on right after it occurred.

That night I read the details, then informed the congregation that we should pray for a solution that would stop the underwater pipe from pouring oil into the Gulf and causing the crisis to continue. The congregation of about 1,500 stood to their feet and prayed with intense fervency and faith.

The environmentalists were warning that this crisis would last for years and cost billions of dollars. To the joy of all of us, a few weeks after the congregation prayed, it was announced that a man had discovered the solution that would seal the underwater pipe. It worked. After the cleanup, businesses once again opened, and the tourist and fishing industry recovered from the storm.

Why did the Holy Spirit give this warning? When a major crisis is coming that will have an economic, spiritual, or emotional impact on His people, the Lord prepares them with a warning. Then through prayer, God can give them a plan of action or a way of escape from the coming calamity (such as with Lot). Lot escaped the destruction of his city by getting out (Gen. 19). Job endured his trial for many months until it ended (Job 42), while Noah patiently rode out a long storm for over a year (Gen. 7-8). In each case, God brought these men through.

Job had his property and blessings restored. Noah and his sons repopulated and rebuilt society. Lot was responsible for a new nation, formed by his sons Edom and Moab, which today is the modern nation of Jordan.

The biblical writer James, when speaking of Job's trial said, "You have seen the end of the Lord." This means that we see how God, in the end, brings people through their negative circumstances. As the warnings unfold, keep in mind that there is a conclusion to all things bad and a beginning for all things new.

CHAPTER 6

THREE TORNADOS AND HILLARY CLINTON

This vision of Hillary Clinton came to pass several years after I saw it. Occasionally I spoke about this during our prophetic conferences. The fulfillment of this vision occurred in 2016 when Clinton ran for President against Donald Trump.

In 2008, Hillary Clinton ran against Barack Obama, hoping to be selected to represent the Democrat Party, but she lost the primary. When Barack Obama became President, he appointed Hillary as Secretary of State. She resigned before continuing into a second term, as her plan was to run in the 2016 election and become President. At the Democrat Convention, she was selected as their candidate, but she unexpectedly lost her bid for the presidency to noted businessman Donald Trump.

Long before she and Trump collided on the campaign trail, I had a detailed vision of her that revealed three storms that would hinder her from winning the election.

The vision began with me standing in a large, downtown city. I stepped into a van with what appeared to be a church youth group. Once I sat in the van, I heard a noise from outside that sounded like a strong wind gusting in the city. My first thought was that a violent storm was brewing, and a tornado or series of tornados would be involved.

The scene immediately changed. I was standing beside a straight road that went as far as the eye could see. There was no traffic on the road, no trees or vegetation in the area, just a very large, open field. There was grass covering the field, but no grains (corn or wheat) of any kind. Standing in the middle of this field was Hillary Clinton, wearing a bright yellow business jacket and matching pants. Up to that point, I had never seen Hillary on television or in any photograph in an outfit that color.

She was making a speech and smiling while making gestures with her hands. In the far distance directly behind her at the end of the field were three extremely tall tornadoes that reached from the ground to the sky. From the ground upward, all three tornados had very thin stems that became larger and wider the higher they reached upward. They were all the same size and height, spaced side by side in an orderly fashion. They were not yet moving toward her, but each one was beginning to spin separately, starting with the one on the left. She was oblivious to the fact that she eventually would be struck from behind by all three tornadoes, about the same time.

As I looked on, I knew that the tornadoes did not represent a coming natural storm, such as a hurricane or tornado in Kansas. Instead, they represented three major problems connected with Hillary's candidacy that were going to sneak up behind her. She would be overtaken suddenly by the violent winds of controversy that would swirl around her. This would be almost like a death, but a political one, not a physical one.

The third scene shifted from Hillary to the outskirts of a major city. In the vision, I was not informed of the city's location. I was standing in a field similar to the one in which I had previously seen Hillary. I looked up into the sky where there were two strange star formations that took on the outlines of two different animals—an alligator and a bear. My first thought was that a bear and alligator could be dangerous animals if they felt threatened. The alligator slowly moves toward its prey, then suddenly opens its mouth and grabs its victim. The bear is a bit different. When a mother bear feels that her cubs or their security are being threatened, she will attack suddenly and violently, and will rip to shreds anyone that she deems a threat.

On several occasions I shared the details of this vision. I remember how shocked I was when someone sent me a color picture of Hillary making a speech. There she was, wearing the same yellow pantsuit I saw her wearing in the field.

So, what were the three tornadoes? From spring to fall of 2016, the year of the presidential election, there were many negative revelations about Clinton, but three different "storms" made national news, and, in my opinion, caused her to lose the election.

The first storm involved newly released details of the horrible 2012 attack on the U.S. consulate in Benghazi, Libya, which resulted in the deaths of four people, including the ambassador. This occurred under Hillary Clinton's watch as Secretary of State. News was eventually released that our government was running weapons from Libya to Turkey, and then to Syrian rebels. A similar scandal called Iran-Contra that involved the sale of weapons sent people to prison during the Reagan administration.

The second storm was the release of financial information which showed that she had sold her influence and government position to raise hundreds of millions of dollars for the Clinton Foundation.

Third was her emails. She used an unsecured server in her home to receive emails, including classified ones, from the State Department. News reports stated that her private server, with State Department emails, had been hacked by a Chinese organization. Then, her emails and those of John Podesta were released by WikiLeaks, revealing that

Hillary appeared to be all that her opponents and detractors claimed she was and more.

I believe it was the combination of these three controversies, as seen in the symbolism of tornados, which blindsided her and possibly impacted the outcome of the 2016 election.

In the visions, the alligator and bear formations were in the sky after the storms hit the field. How would an alligator or bear sitting in the heavens (a high position) come into play?

A widespread symbol for Russia is the bear. After it appeared that Hillary might lose to Donald Trump, corrupt people in high positions immediately began a united effort to use their political influence to investigate Trump and his alleged ties to Russia. For two years after he was elected, the media hammered us incessantly with their Russia collusion stories until we were revolted by it. Congress appointed a special counsel and spent tens of millions of dollars to investigate a false claim of Russia collusion. Time has since revealed that this false story was orchestrated behind the scenes and paid for by the Clinton campaign and others.

Alligators often symbolize verbal attacks. Just as a vicious alligator will kill with the power of its mouth, so the politicians and the media, sitting in their high places, used their mouths in their attempts to politically kill Donald Trump.

I told these visions publicly on several occasions. However, the interpretation was not fully understood until events transpired prior to and after the election. I share this vision to demonstrate how the Holy Spirit knew what was coming long before events unfolded.

One purpose for a warning dream or vision is to reveal information in advance that is already known in the Spirit realm. God reveals future events in detail to prove that He alone is the God who can reveal secrets. Paul wrote that the Holy Spirit reveals the secrets of men's hearts (1 Cor. 14:25). Daniel noted that there is a God in heaven who reveals secrets, and He makes known to you what shall come to pass (Dan. 2:28-29).

For some reason, many politicians believe they can outsmart the system, bribe inner circle friends who will protect their corruption, and collect so much blackmail dirt on their colleagues that those in political circles dare not touch, expose, or speak negatively about their actions for fear of retaliation. Yet, if you could interview Nebuchadnezzar, the former king of Babylon, he would inform you that pride will always become a leader's downfall. This proud and wealthy king spent seven years living in a field like a beast with his political clout stripped from him (Dan. 4). Only when he humbled himself, repented of pride, and turned his heart to God was his throne restored.

We have all seen how some believe they are above justice and sit on a throne above the Most High God. However, when God lifts His hand to releases His storms, even the highest can be brought low. This should be a lesson to each of us.

CHAPTER 7

VISION OF EMPTY CITIES AND STREETS

The following vision remained with me and was burned into my mind and spirit, to the point that at least once a week, I would recall this vision and ponder the meaning. What I saw and warned others about did not come to pass for many years. At the time that the Holy Spirit showed me the details, I could only speculate about how the strange events that I saw would unfold.

This was a full color vision that is as clear today as the moment it occurred. It started out with me riding in an SUV with several ministry team members, heading out to one of our conferences, which at that time were held in large churches or convention centers. When preparing for the larger meetings, our ministry team would pack equipment and ministry resources in large, rectangular Anvil cases on wheels. Several times a year, four to eight of these large cases were loaded onto a large truck, then driven to the conference location. At the time of this vision, our ministry was hosting four large conferences every year in different places.

In this vision, I was preparing to set up a conference in a city that had large, high, downtown office buildings. As we approached the city, the vehicle I was in suddenly came to a complete stop. We all got out to inspect the problem and noticed that all four wheels were missing from the vehicle, making it impossible to travel. We were simply *stuck* in one spot.

I looked in the direction of the city and noticed my four black Anvil cases in one straight line. When I tried to push the first one in the direction of the city, the wheels fell off, making it impossible to move. I opened the first case, and inside I saw a beautiful, long-stemmed silver trumpet. I set the trumpet to my mouth to sound a loud blast, but no sound came out. The trumpet was silent.

Immediately, I opened the second case, which concealed another trumpet that I attempted to blow. As with the first, no sound came out. I found myself lifting the large lid on the third case, only to find another trumpet identical to the other two silver trumpets. For the third time, no sound could be produced by blowing into the trumpet. By the time I opened the fourth case, the strong cases began to fall apart. I attempted to take the long stems of the trumpets and combine them as one big trumpet, but the sound of the fourth trumpet was silent. I understood that there would be no meetings for an extended period, and I would not be traveling.

The real shocker came when I laid down the fourth trumpet and turned toward the vehicle. It had turned into bones – not metal, but bones, as though it became a corpse. I began to move the cases that were now on one side of the road so that nobody would be hurt if they passed by.

I then looked toward the large, beautiful buildings in the city ahead of us. All were perfectly intact. The sun was shining and the sky was blue. It appeared to be a normal day. Yet, there was nobody on the streets. The sidewalks were empty with not a single person in sight. I also noticed there were no cars anywhere, not on any road, nor entering or exiting the city. There was no evidence of public transportation, such as taxis or buses. It was a beautiful day in broad daylight,

VISION OF EMPTY CITIES AND STREETS

yet there were no signs of human activities. There was only silence in every direction.

Based on the trumpets being silent, my vehicle being tireless, and empty cities, I knew that my ministry travel schedule would one day be completely interrupted, as it would not be possible to conduct large ministry events. No sound coming from the trumpets indicated no messages would be heard. At the last scene, I turned to my travel vehicle. The tires were on it, but the engine was missing.

For many years, I struggled to understand what event or crisis could take place that would shut down entire cities. My only thought was an extreme interruption in the fuel supplies, to the point that all forms of transportation had to stop. If gas prices rose astronomically, if people were unable to afford fuel, or if no fuel was available, then perhaps a shutdown would occur. Based upon what I knew about the oil supply and our national oil reserves, this interpretation made little sense.

Because this was a vision, as clear as the 9-11 vision I had experienced in Florida, I knew I would see it play out in the future.

THE DAY IT OCCURRED

In the winter of 2019, Covid-19 quickly spread from China into other nations, causing sickness and death. In March and April of 2020, over 16,000 youth were registered for our Warrior-Fest conferences at the Omega Center International. By early spring, the government was forcing lockdowns and limiting gatherings to no more than fifty people, then no more than twenty people. Soon gatherings were restricted to no more than ten people at one time.

Despite the setbacks, both Warrior-Fest events were conducted over the Internet as our team ministered in a roomful of empty seats in a building that seats 3,500. Despite an empty building, over 50,000 individuals viewed each event online.

By early summer, ministry partners were sending us pictures of Atlanta, Birmingham, and New York City. Shockingly, there in picture form was the fulfillment of the vision! Downtown streets were empty. Hotels, restaurants, and shops were closed. Not one person was walking on the street, in broad daylight! Millions were told to work from home, and public schools were closed. Large cities were on lockdowns. Our normal daily routines were gone, and life was virtually at a standstill.

For several months I was unable to travel. That explained the wheels falling off the cases and the SUV without an engine. Recalling the vehicle turn to bones reminded me of the hearse that carries the corpses of deceased virus victims to their final resting places.

My hectic and nonstop ministry traveling schedule came to a screeching halt. I spent my time off the road in the form of a much-needed sabbatical. The time leading up to April 2021 was a reset for me personally and for our ministry. Without a doubt, the impact of covid on the world was the fulfillment of this vision.

THE 18-WHEELER WITHOUT WHEELS

With the discussion in this section on transportation, I'll tell a quick vision I had in the early fall of 2020. During prayer, as I was sitting back in my prayer chair, I clearly saw the left side of an 18-wheel tractor-trailer. I did not see the cab where the driver sits, but I did observe the long rig of the truck. All I saw was this single truck, nothing else. Slowly, the tires vanished from the entire truck.

My mind immediately went back to the vision of the tires missing from my vehicle, which alluded to a cessation of travel. It is not always possible to know the meanings and impact of certain dreams or visions in advance. But if I were to say what I believe this indicates, it would be a warning of some type of delay or hindrance that causes the trucking industry to be unable to deliver their products.

There are an untold number of problems that could hinder or delay delivery trucks. There is talk of a rubber supply shortage, from which tires are made. An earthquake could make roads and bridges impass- able. Various problems could raise fuel prices to unaffordable levels or reduce supplies altogether. Violence in cities could shut down trucking to those areas. A trucking strike could continue for an extended period.

As I write this, cargo ships are stuck in the Atlantic and Pacific Oceans with goods being imported to America, and the ships are not permitted into port. Cargo that trucks would transport is still on the ships. We are being told that this problem will not be resolved for another year, which would bring us to the fall of 2022.

At this point we don't know exactly how this vision will come to pass. Again, time will be the interpreter.

WARNINGS PREPARE US

Any warning vision we receive is not to *scare* us, but to *prepare* us. In both Testaments, God provided prophetic warnings to prepare His people. In Acts 11:28, Agabus, a noted prophet in the early church, warned the Christians in Judea that a terrible famine was coming to the world. This happened in the days of Claudius Caesar. Paul raised offerings throughout his ministry to provide relief to the churches before famines and difficulties arrived. The warning of the coming famine was so that Christians could set in motion a plan of action for the churches to unite and provide relief for those in need. The rule of *warning for preparation* still applies today.

CHAPTER 8

VISIONS OF CITIES BURNING

The following vision involved American cities, and it has been fulfilled in part. However, there are other aspects of the vision that I believe are yet to come. I did not write down the exact year that this vision occurred, but the date on the original paper is May 8. Our ministry was conducting a conference in Pigeon Forge, Tennessee, and my family was staying in a hotel room at the Smoky Mountain Conference Center.

This vision came to me while I was asleep. It was not a dream, because it was very bold and clear. The vision opened with me standing on the banks of a large, winding river. The events unfolded sometime in the night, as darkness surrounded the cities. I could see the city lights from at least five (perhaps up to seven) different skylines of major cities. The activities that were developing appeared to be in downtown areas, located between tall office buildings or skyscrapers. Throughout the vision, I was unaware of the geographical location of any of these cities, not even the state or states where the cities were located.

Suddenly, I saw extreme violence break out. People were fighting, rioting, breaking windows, and burning cars, and it spread throughout these cities. Fires were occurring in various parts of each city as rioters set buildings aflame. When the fires and rioting began in the first city, the violence and burning soon spread to other cities. The dark sky lit up with a red-orange glow. I stood at this river and turned my body

180 degrees as I watched these cities in crisis. I understood in the vision that some of the areas where the fires were originating were in the poorer sections of the city.

RIOTS BEGAN IN 2020

Years later, in 2020, America encountered great civil unrest from radical far-left groups such as ANTIFA, resulting in violence that included rioting, looting, and arson. By summer that year, some cities had imposed curfews. Between one and two billion dollars in damage and theft costs were incurred. Cities with the highest levels of violence included Minneapolis, Portland, Kenosha, New York City, Louisville, Seattle, and Chicago. Most of these riots were civil unrest due to racial conflicts, some involving actions of a local police officer.

DAVID WILKERSON'S VISIONS

I believe that my vision of the burning cities has partially occurred, and will also have a future fulfillment. There may be more unrest coming, especially for New York City. One reason I say this is because of the visions of Pastor David Wilkerson.

Years ago, David Wilkerson, a powerful man of God and a true prophetic voice for America, had a series of visions in which he saw, among other things, massive fires break out across New York City. In this section I have written his warnings from articles and newsletters he wrote, and from messages to his church at Times Square.

On September 7, 1992, David wrote about seeing 1,000 fires in New York:

"I have had a recurring vision of over 1,000 fires burning at one time in New York City. I am convinced race riots will soon explode. New York is right now a powder keg, ready to blow. Federal and state welfare cutbacks will be the spark that ignites the fuse... 100,000 angry men will be on the streets, enraged because they have been cut off from benefits... fires will rage everywhere...."

He reported again in March 2009:

"An earth-shattering calamity is about to happen...it is going to be frightening...we are all going to tremble, even the godliest among us... Major cities all across America will experience riots and blazing fires, such as we saw in Watts, Los Angeles years ago... There will be riots and fires in cities worldwide... there will be looting...."

A close friend of Pastor Wilkerson said that the minister told him privately that one warning of the fires was from an angel of the Lord. However, he refused to say it publicly, as people were so full of unbelief and skepticism that many would only mock. This warning of fires in New York City, massive rioting, and looting was recorded and stated publicly on several different occasions over the years, prior to Pastor's tragic death in a car accident on April 27, 2011.

As I have stated, a vision revealed does not necessarily mean it is about to occur immediately. My experience has been that the vision is an advance warning that may not occur for years or even decades. The book of Revelation is about future events, and the vision is over 1,900 years old!

Over the years, Christians who are familiar with David Wilkerson's visions have asked me what I personally believe could trigger such a crisis in New York City. I cannot speak for Wilkerson, but I can suggest a few possibilities from discussions, research, and observations.

1. The Bankruptcy of Cities

With the covid outbreaks, many businesses in major cities and entire states were forced by their government leaders to close. There was little to no income for shops, restaurants, and other small businesses, which in turn impacted wages, jobs, and tax revenue. According to a 2019 Forbes report, out of seventy-five of America's most populous cities, sixty-three do not have enough money to pay their bills. And that was *before* the government shut down sources of revenue.

The federal government is in even worse shape, with spending and debt at astronomically high levels and the inflation rate rising daily. A bankrupt city, state, and federal government may not be able to provide any kind of assistance to the citizens, which in turn could trigger violent protests.

2. Job Losses

The unemployment rate fluctuates based upon economic growth or business decline. By fall of 2020, close to 100,000 businesses had permanently shut their doors after being forced to close during covid shutdowns. Others who remained open have seen their revenues sharply decline. Millions of people have transitioned to shopping online, thus affecting in-person shopping and businesses. Even large, well-known retail businesses closed some or all of their stores. Portions of large shopping malls are sitting empty.

Government financial assistance during 2020 and 2021 created a shortage of workers for many retail stores, small businesses and fast-food chains, because people were making more money staying home than they could have made working.

Natural disasters such as hurricanes, tornados, and floods also destroy homes, businesses, and livelihoods. When Hurricane Ida struck off the coast of Louisiana, it damaged or destroyed more than 22,000 power poles and 5,200 transformers. The staggering level of devastation caused weeks-long electricity outages and shortages of water, fuel, and necessary supplies. Imagine the kind of chain reaction this could cause in a place such as New York City.

3. Inability to Pay Debts or Retirement

A third possibility is the inability for a city to pay retirement pensions for employees of the city government. Many cities and states can no longer afford the unsustainable retirement promises they made to millions of public workers. The solution offered was to increase taxes, divert other funds, or persuade workers to relinquish money they are owed. In some cities, such as Chicago, the city only had thirty percent of what was needed to cover municipal workers. Other cities have sold bonds with interest they are unable to pay. Leaders of certain cities or states then look to the federal government to bail them out.

This type of crisis in a place like New York City, with a population of over 8.8 million people, could be a recipe for a violent clash with the working class.

4. Cut Back on Government Benefits

In a large city, you will always find people who are on some form of government financial assistance. It might be rental assistance, food stamps, welfare, and so on. I certainly hope that those truly in need can and will continue to be helped in whatever manner possible.

However, if our federal and state governments face a hyperinflation crisis, such as that of the German Weimar Republic in the 1920s, our country is in trouble. We are already following their path as our government excessively spends money we don't have, keeps printing money with nothing to back it, and pays people not to work. If US fiat currency becomes worthless due to hyperinflation, America's cities will become the epicenter of pain and anger expressed by large numbers of people.

National and international economic experts are warning that the U.S. Federal Reserve and Treasury Department cannot continue down this monetary path without massively increasing taxes, productivity, and export income. Our own government is debasing our currency and causing hyperinflation, thus reducing the purchasing power of our dollar. Something that would normally cost one dollar could rise to ten dollars or even fifty dollars in one year. This occurred in Germany, and wheelbarrows full of money were worthless.

Any major disruption in government relief programs, such as Social Security, welfare checks, or food stamps, as well as the inability for people to purchase necessary goods because they are unaffordable, would enrage the needy and send tens of thousands into the streets protesting. As in the past, there likely would be looting, rioting, and burning of property.

5. Another Terrorist Attack

On September 11, 2001, New York City experienced the emotional, physical, and economic impact of a deadly terrorist attack. Thousands of innocent lives were sent into eternity. The economic impact resulted in the loss of 143,000 jobs per month over a three-month period. The jobs represented industries such as finance, professional services, the arts, management, and manufacturing. Billions were lost in wages from September 11 to December 11. My family personally knew someone whose company closed after 9/11 because the investor had hundreds of millions of dollars in bonds that were like cash at a financial company located in the World Trade Center. When the towers fell, the money literally went up in smoke and could not be replaced. The company never reopened.

If another assault of this magnitude occurred in New York City, the stress from months of lockdowns, closure of businesses, and economic turmoil could cause people to snap under emotional stress.

Over the years, I have spoken with military and intelligence personnel who specialize in counterterrorism operations. I have asked them what their greatest concerns are for America's largest cities. Many point out that New York City is the primary target, as it is viewed globally as a representation of America's financial and economic strength.

Several counterterrorism experts have mentioned four possible terror attacks. One concern is that a small nuclear bomb or a dirty bomb created from radioactive materials could be carried in a suitcase and detonated. Several years ago, it was confirmed that a particular country was in possession of suitcase-sized nuclear bombs that would destroy and radiate several city blocks. I was told that our intelligence believed that some were missing and had perhaps been purchased on the black market by Islamic radicals in Pakistan or Afghanistan.

The second concern would be an electro-magnetic pulse (EMP). This is a bomb that, if detonated in the atmosphere, would create a pulse of energy that would temporarily or permanently damage electronics and anything with semiconductor components. This type of bomb could be released from a cargo ship sitting in the sea, just off our coast. A member of the military explained to me that the EMP affects copper wiring, which would affect anything with a computer, as well as the power grid, water filtering systems, underground subways, and all transportation. Most individuals in New York City live in high rise apartments and eat in diners and restaurants. A news network noted that most people living in the city have only a one-day supply of food. Even restaurants and diners are resupplied each day by trucks bringing in food.

I asked this gentleman how a place like New York City would look if an EMP were released. He replied that it would be like living in the days before there was electricity. It could take two years to recover because so many things that people depend on would become useless. Even a low orbiting satellite that is not hardened against an EMP would be useless.

We do know that terrorist organizations have studied the use of an EMP and have discussed the possibility of one day releasing such a device over America or one of our major cities. The idea to strike America with such a weapon was reported in the Iranian Military Journal during the Obama administration. An EMP is a real threat. According to the State Department, a certain sized bomb released over the central United States would destroy most of the electronics in the entire Continental United States.

The third event that keeps some experts awake at night is the possibility of an attack on America's old power grid. In the past, foreign powers have hacked the power grid, and the grid continues to be vulnerable to cyberattacks. Without electrical power, America would be brought to her knees in a matter of days.

6. Fuel Problems

The fourth event involves fuel. In 1973, OPEC issued an oil embargo against the United States, in retaliation for helping supply Israel with weapons during the 1973 war with Egypt and Syria. The price of fuel at the pump skyrocketed, and the last number of your license plate determined the day that you were allowed to sit in a long line and buy gasoline. We lived in Northern Virginia at the time, and I remember the long lines at the gas stations. Drivers wasted gasoline sitting in long lines waiting to fill up their tanks.

Under President Trump, America became energy independent because of important energy-related decisions he made. Soon after taking office, Joe Biden shut down the Keystone pipeline and made other decisions that cost thousands of jobs through a ripple effect and immediately raised the price of fuel.

There is a strong push to stop producing fossil fuel vehicles and replace them with electric vehicles. That brings its own set of challenges. Where will all these electric cars be charged? What kind of fuel is needed to produce the electricity needed to charge all those electric cars? What are batteries made of? What is required to mine lithium to produce so many expensive car batteries? Who owns the lithium, and who makes money off selling it? Is there a great financial incentive for the people pushing electric cars? How long does a battery last? What happens when the expensive battery must be replaced? How do you travel when a storm or other disaster has cut power for days or weeks and you can't charge your car battery?

We have already witnessed the burning of cities. However, with numerous types of possible terrorist attacks, natural disasters, federal and state budget concerns, and racially charged incidents, the burning of major cities continues to be a strong possibility.

In Lot's day, four cities burned and one little city, Zoar, escaped devastation. The town was on a high mountain that overlooked the four cities in the valley. Lot and his two daughters were instructed by two angelic messengers to get to the mountain to avoid what was coming. In Revelation, we read where men will flee and hide themselves in the mountains and dens (Rev. 6:15).

Any individual or family living in a major U.S. city must weigh the high-income benefits and the conveniences of city life against the various dangers that could unfold, especially in cities that are a bullseye for trouble. No place can guarantee 100% safety and security, especially during a surge of disasters. However, there are sections of the country that tend to be safer than others. These locations are often smaller towns and communities with a strong Christian population. Listen to and obey the Holy Spirit, and you might protect yourself from danger ahead.

VISIONS FROM FROM FRED STONE'S JOURNALS

CHAPTER 9

AN EAST COAST NUCLEAR ATTACK

M y father was a pastor and occasionally a traveling evangelist. He passed away in March of 2011. Those who sat under
his ministry knew him to be a powerful, yet humble man
of God, and one who fasted and prayed often. He was blessed to operate
in several spiritual gifts (1 Cor. 12:7-10). To this day, we hear testimo-
nies from people Dad prayed for who received some form of healing.

Dad was also known for receiving meaningful spiritual dreams,
including warning dreams. Perhaps the most shocking and dramatic
experience during his lifetime occurred when he was pastoring in
Troutman, North Carolina. I heard him relate this encounter with
fear and trembling on several occasions. A few years ago, I found the
original paper Dad had written on the night the encounter occurred.
What he saw that night has not yet happened. He said he hoped that
God had heard our prayers and prevented the horrific attack. Still, we
were aware, from both Scripture and experience, that a warning vision
might not come to pass for many years or even generations.

The paper Dad wrote this on was dated January 5, 1982, and the
time was 3:20 a.m. It is significant to add here that, when I was in my
pre-teen and early-teen years, Dad pastored a church in Alexandria,
Virginia, outside the District of Columbia. Some high-level government

employees attended our church, including men who worked for the CIA. They sometimes confided in Dad. One man told Dad about the Watergate break-in, days before it was reported by the Washington Post. He predicted that President Nixon would resign.

The following is detailed information that Dad related about his experience in 1982:

It was very late, and I had been reading in the bedroom. I heard the front door open and thought it was my son Phillip coming home from shift work. I saw someone near the doorway of the bedroom, and I realized it was not Phillip, but a well-dressed man. For some reason I was not afraid. I spoke up and said, "Can I help you? Do you need something?" He replied, "I have been sent here to give you some information."

I told him to go into my office, which was down the hall. I sat down at the desk and reached for a pen and paper to write down the information. The man never came into the office but stood just outside the doorway. He spoke as I wrote.

"Russian nuclear services will strike a major American city without warning. The Russians will have a naval fleet that is hiding near Bermuda and Haiti. They also will be 25 miles off the Baltimore-Chesapeake Bay area. They go undetected because of heavy sea traffic. There will also be one sub about 2 miles off the Boston area, and one off the Florida coast. They will perfect a system that they believe will enable them to go undetected by the American forces.

"Their plan is to use heavy radiation missiles for maximum kill and confusion. The Russian Naval Intelligence is banking on their naval submarine strike forces to be undetected. Their plan is for the United States government to capitulate to prevent an all-out nuclear war. Thus far the Russian sub-force crews have come ashore in all staging areas, undetected, for R and R and social training tests. Allied intelligence can check out crew members if a proper check on English speaking crew members is made. So far, they have been 100% successful in purchasing food, drinks, and reading materials."

When Dad asked how the men in the submarines could come ashore without being detected, the man answered:

"The Russians have fishing trawlers in international waters. At times the fishing trawlers will group together over the area of a submarine. The sub will surface and the men, dressed in common clothes, will access the boats. This was a technique developed to assist the men in being undetected. All of the men on the boats can speak perfect English."

The man told how, over the years, Soviet KGB agents, posing as students in large universities, took sea maps showing the location of barrier reefs and passed the information on to the Soviet naval authorities. Certain reefs were of such a nature that a sub could not be detected except by U.S. naval forces using a slanted detection system. The subs were sitting on barrier reefs in such a location that sonar, as normally used, could not detect it. Moving out to sea, they must search at a 45-degree angle. The barrier reef extends over the sitting sub, protecting it from exposure to surface ships.

He informed Dad that our intelligence forces can detect the Russian subs if they follow movements closely. He said that some of the crew call themselves "Soviet Knights" because of the years they believe they have gone undetected. The man said, "Their code name is Michael Atlantic."

In a final question Dad asked the man, "Why have you come to tell me this?" The man replied:

> *"There are secret Christians on these ships who are concerned about a possible strike in the future. They have been praying, asking that the submarines be exposed to someone in the government. One of the men now working on a sub visited your church in Northern Virginia. He remembered you and asked God to show you what is coming."*

The man gave Dad the name of someone in Washington DC and told him to write a letter to this man and give all the details he had just received. He stated that this man would be one of the only people who would believe that a minister actually received a supernatural visitation and warning. Dad did write the letter, although he never received a response to my knowledge.

Dad wrote the last words, laid down the pen, and suddenly began to weep. He spoke to the man, but there was silence from the hallway. Dad stood up to find him, but nobody was there. He checked both doors and they were locked. He was uncertain if he had experienced a startling vision, similar to the type that Peter experienced in Acts 10. Or was it possible that God had sent an angelic messenger in the form of a man to bring this warning?

CONFIRMED IN CALIFORNIA

Years later, I was preaching in Orange County, California at the Westminster Church of God. For some reason, I shared the above experience with the entire congregation. Present that night was a man who was active in US Naval Intelligence. He asked to speak with me.

He said, "I am not able to tell you the information I know. Let me just say, what that man said to your father was accurate."

This visitation occurred in 1982. The year 2022 would make it forty years ago. The number 40 in scripture marks a generation of unbelief (Psa. 95:10). Without a doubt, the United States has entered a dangerous spiritual stage of utter unbelief and callousness of heart.

For many years, various servants of God have seen dreams or visions of mushroom clouds over major cities in America or missiles being shot out of the sea. Some have gone so far as to say that this is how America will meet its demise.

My father was living when the events of 9-11 occurred. From that horrific day, until the day he departed this life, he earnestly interceded, sometimes every day, asking the Almighty to expose terrorist attacks and not allow the plans of evil men to succeed. I remember having dinner with a former US Senator who served during the George W. Bush administration. He told me the number of terrorist attacks that had been thwarted across the United States. When I told Dad, tears came to his eyes.

Although Dad never heard back from the man he contacted in Washington, we hope someone followed up as a result of the letter. I have hoped and prayed that this attack would be prevented once it was exposed. As I continually teach, time is the interpreter of prophecies and visions.

CHAPTER 10

WARNING WASHINGTON OF TERRORIST ATTACKS

I n this chapter I am sharing information that my father was hesitant to tell publicly. Dad never wanted to be known as someone
who received special spiritual gifts or revelations from God. He
did, however, have a God-given gift that, at times, enabled him to see
events before they happened. I know of direct and detailed warnings he
gave friends and church members. In this example, he had a national
warning for the government.

This vision occurred about one month after the September 11
terrorist attacks. Dad and I were ministering one weekend at Pace
Assembly in Pace, Florida. We were staying at a local Hampton Inn.
When we awoke Saturday morning, Dad was greatly troubled. He told
me that he had a strange vision in which he saw a terror cell preparing
an attack on the Treasury Building in Washington, DC. I will not tell
the details of what Dad saw the terrorists planning, as it was a bril-
liant idea that would go undetected until it was too late. The group
was secretly preparing their attack in a barn on a piece of property in
Maryland.

Because of Dad's reputation to see things before they occurred,
when he had a vision or dream related to government or the nation, he
would receive calls from a man in the FBI who was a believer. This man

carefully listened to Dad's dreams and visions. Dad's reputation was known among some in the highest levels of our government, including at one time the President of the United States.

That morning at breakfast, he asked me if there was anyone I could contact in the highest levels of the federal government to warn of the plot he saw. I knew of one woman whose daughter was the secretary to the head of a Cabinet in the Bush administration. Both were believers. I called this woman and put Dad on the phone. He gave her the details of this troubling vision and asked her to please get word to whomever she could, and tell them what was being planned.

The woman contacted her daughter. Soon after, we received a call from this same woman. She said, "My daughter took the information to her boss, and they both met with the President this morning at a briefing. The President said they knew there was another attack planned on Washington, but they were unaware of the target." She told us to watch the news, because they are going to act on your dad's warning, not as a vision from a preacher, but as a tip from a reliable source. Indeed, we watched the news and saw that the streets were being blocked in certain areas to prevent this attack.

Years later, another woman who was a student at Regent University in Virginia Beach, Virginia sent us a letter. She wrote that the former Attorney General had spoken at the university and relayed the story of a southern minister who had a vision and gave a warning that was accurate while he was serving in in the administration. She said, "I think he was speaking about your dad without naming him." I teared up a bit, knowing that my dad, who came from a small town in the mountains of West Virginia, had been used of God on a national level.

A WARNING TO THE PRESIDENT

Dad and I were ministering at a great church in Augusta, Georgia during President George W. Bush's second term. Hours before sunrise, Dad suddenly awoke and turned on the television. I was in the same hotel room but was unaware of what was happening until morning. Dad said, "Son, I had a vision last night that was so real, I got up and turned on the news to see if something happened to President Bush!"

He gave me the details:

"Air Force One had landed in a foreign nation. The President walked down the steps, and the Secret Service agents stood around him as he entered his vehicle. Suddenly, two men nearby who were security agents for another world leader pulled their weapons and shot the President. I saw Bush drop as the Secret Service began pulling guns and shooting at the men.

"I then saw Fox News with a breaking story that the President had been assassinated. The news was blaming the Secret Service and spoke of them being in the wrong position to protect the president. [Dad knew the name that the Secret Service called that particular position, because it was revealed in the vision.] I also heard the code name of the place Bush was planning to be for this meeting. The name was Shangri-La."

Using the same contact, Dad's detailed vision was given to someone who had direct access to President George W. Bush. Later we received a call telling us the message had been received. We were told that President Bush was amazed and concerned, especially upon hearing the name Shangri-La. There was one location overseas where they used the code name Shangri-La! He had a meeting planned for the area, and I understand that he gave instructions to cancel it.

On several occasions, one of President Bush's close personal friends from Knoxville, Tennessee gave the President letters that I wrote wherein Dad or I relayed dreams or visions. We were told that the President took the information seriously.

VISION OF THE CAPITOL ATTACK

I remind the reader that a vision is for an appointed time, and though it tarry, wait for it, because it will surely come (Hab. 2:2-3). Dad taught me that any warning in a spiritual dream or vision should be taken seriously and prayed over, especially if you sense a strong burden connected with the warning.

One vision Dad experienced involved the US Capitol. In this vision, he saw both sides of the Capitol building in Washington, DC. It appeared to be a normal day, and nothing in the vision gave evidence of what was coming.

Suddenly there was a very loud explosion inside the Capitol. Dad was uncertain if it originated within the building, or if some type of missile had been shot from the other side and entered the historic structure. He could hear screams and sirens filling the air. He saw members of Congress whom he recognized that were burned, and others had died in the blast.

He could hear what sounded like news commentators calling the explosion a well-planned terrorist attack. Dad said the dream changed, and in a room that seemed to be in an abandoned building, he saw a group of men making a bomb. There was a colored liquid in what appeared to be glass containers. He assumed that this may have been the material used to create the explosive device. He also sensed that, to accomplish this, there had been assistance from personnel within the Capitol itself.

Dad described the scene as utter chaos. He repeated this to me several times with great concern. Dad loved this country and was always praying against any type of terrorist attack being planned. His prayer was to expose the plots and plans to the proper sources, in hopes of preventing any attack from being carried out. This attack has not yet occurred, and hopefully, prayer and intercession can expose it before it does.

Sometimes, an attack or a judgment can be delayed. In 2 Kings chapter 19, when 185,000 Assyrian troops surrounded Jerusalem, King Hezekiah and Isaiah joined in intense prayer, interceding for a reprieve and divine intervention from God. When the sun rose, the entire Assyrian army was dead, apparently from some type of strange plague. Nineveh was on God's hit list to be overtaken by an invading army within forty days if the city did not repent. Through the warning and preaching of the rebellious prophet Jonah, the people of Nineveh repented and turned from their wickedness, and the city was spared for 150 years. These are examples of attacks and judgments being delayed through repentance and prayer.

I am sharing these past events to encourage and help readers understand that God still speaks to His children today in many ways, including through His written Word, through the inner voice of His Spirit, and through spiritual dream and visions. This should be an encouragement to all intercessors that the Almighty uses the foolish things of this world to confound the wise (1 Cor. 1:27). He makes the common things uncommon. A résumé of the biblical prophets indicates that these men came from backgrounds that included fishermen, farmers, shepherds, nomads, cup bearers, and tax collectors. All the Almighty needs is an ear in tune to hear.

CHAPTER 11

DIMINISHED FOOD SUPPLIES

S everal months prior to my father's death, I spent some time with him at his home. He was sitting in a recliner and invited me to sit next to him on the couch. He had something important to tell me.

He looked troubled as he said, "I saw something very strange last night. It was somewhat of a dream-vision. I was standing outside, looking at the front yard. I saw three sets of knives, forks, and spoons. However, one set was buried in the ground and only two sets were above ground."

He asked me what I thought the scene represented. I responded, "The utensils are used when a person eats a meal. The average family will eat three meals a day—breakfast, lunch, and dinner. Something is buried underground when it dies. I believe the scene is revealing that a third of either the world or America's food supply will be gone or diminished. It will impact our three daily meals."

He nodded his head in agreement and commented, "That's exactly what I believe the interpretation is."

For the food supply in America to be diminished by one third, at least one or a combination of the following would likely occur:

- A serious drought that destroys crops or prevents farming

- The water provided for irrigating crops being reduced by drought or other means

- Farmers losing income, to the point of giving up their farms, thus reducing food supplies

- Delivery trucks being unable or refusing to deliver food to locations.

According to a New York Times report, in the year 2021, much of the western United States experienced the worst drought conditions in centuries. We are told this was caused by the lack of snowfall that would normally melt to replenish lakes and rivers, the lack of rain, and the record heat in some areas. Water is evaporating above ground, and underground water being tapped into is diminishing the reserves.

In California, one almond farmer uprooted his entire farm due to drought. Lake Mead and other freshwater lakes became so low that the drinking water provided for seven states and serving millions of people was in danger of drying up. As of the time this was written, US drought monitor maps show that around half of the United States, particularly the western third of the country, is experiencing abnormally dry to extreme or exceptional drought conditions. It is clear to see how this could create shortages of a third of our food supply if these conditions persist.

Other problems could impact agriculture. In farming states such as Iowa, winter rains have been washing away the rich, black topsoil into the streams and rivers. The bee population is dwindling or disappearing in some states, and bees are necessary for pollination of a wide range of crops. Any natural disasters, such as a major earthquake in the Midwest or along the west coast, or an eruption from a volcano such as Yellowstone, could negatively affect farming and crops. A volcanic eruption could form a dangerous ash cloud that we are told could cover large swathes of America's farmland, making the soil useless for planting and harvesting indefinitely.

Ash alone is dangerous for other reasons. Experts say that the falling volcanic ash would accumulate up to ten feet in some areas and block the sun. Breathing the ash cuts the lungs and hardens like cement. It would kill animals and livestock. A volcanic eruption in that part of the country would have the potential to devastate the food supply.

The federal government is creating another set of problems by providing incentives for farmers to take farmland out of production. This program has been in effect for over thirty years, and the government claims they are doing this to reduce greenhouse gas emissions by 2030. Less farm production means less food being grown, and less food being grown means less food available in the grocery markets.

Plants need carbon dioxide to survive, and globalists and other climate change radicals seem determined to destroy grass, trees, and crops by reducing carbon dioxide emissions to zero. The plan is to starve humans in their bizarre efforts to "save the planet" from humans.

Globalists in the United States and around the world are also determined to stop people from eating meat because they think this will save the earth from carbon dioxide and greenhouse gases. They want us to eat lab-grown meat, but only as an occasional treat. Cattle farmers who raise and feed the livestock are making so little money when they sell the livestock, while the meat processing plants are charging so much money that the globalists hope the farmers will stop raising cattle because the cost isn't worth the effort.

At the time of this writing, we are encountering a completely different problem with the supply chain. This is something we never would have imagined we would see in this country. Food processing companies are facing shortages, and of course this impacts grocery stores and consumers. There seems to be no valid reason for these supply chain problems, and it even appears to be intentionally created to negatively affect consumers and the economy.

I believe that Dad received a warning for the future about the food supply, and we possibly are on the verge of seeing this vision come to pass. Again, time is an interpreter of such events. These types of warnings remind me of Pharaoh's dream. When the famine warning was revealed, a seven-year grace period provided time for Joseph to direct a harvesting plan and set aside grain during seven years of plenty. Often these types of warnings are given years in advance to provide time for planning and preparation.

In the time of King Hezekiah, Isaiah warned Jerusalem of a future Babylonian invasion (Isa. 39:5-7), which did not happen until 150 years later. A delayed warning is not a denied event.

VISIONS NOT YET FULFILLED

CHAPTER 12

TERRORIST ATTACK ON A PUBLIC SCHOOL

Several years after my father passed away, I had an experience that began as a vivid dream. As the dream progressed, it turned into a series of scenes that I classify as a vision.

A few times I have dreamed of Dad, and in those dreams he would say something important or give me a warning. I want to make something clear: if you dream of a loved one who has passed away and you communicate in the dream, that is *not* "talking to the dead," as some allege. It is not some form of attempted communication with the departed. I consider it the same type of vision that Christ experienced when Moses and Elijah appeared to Him on the Mount of Transfiguration (Matt. 17:1-9). Moses had been dead and buried 1,500 year earlier, and Elijah had been taken alive into heaven. Both men spoke to Christ, telling Him about His future death in Jerusalem. Christ called this encounter a *vision*. Many people reading this have dreamed of being with a loved one who has passed away, which is not uncommon.

In the first phase of this dream, I entered a room that reminded me of a public school classroom. There were no students in the room or in the hallways. Dad was sitting in a chair, dressed in his traditional dark suit. His countenance appeared troubled. It reminded me of the serious look he would have after experiencing a troubling dream. I asked him what was wrong.

He said to me, "They have attacked a public school full of children in the town!" Dad then described to me the location of the school where the attack had occurred (which I will not name). A group of terrorists organized a plan to attack the facility during school hours. They had slain or wounded hundreds of children in this one location. It was being called the worst attack since 9-11. For wisdom's sake, there are parts of this I will not tell.

In the vision, because of this attack, Lee University in Cleveland had sent their students back home for fear of being the next target. I spoke to two male college students who chose to remain in town to assist in counseling youth who were traumatized by the attack.

A MEETING WITH THE MAYOR

This vision troubled my spirit for many months. Finally, I requested a private meeting with one of the mayors (we have two—a city and a county) and the Chief of Police. We met privately in my office. I first handed them my book on dreams and visions, explaining how God uses both to bring to light unknown information and warnings. I shared a few brief stories about Dad's warnings that had come to pass. I then related to them about the school shooting vision, giving them the details of what and how it occurred. While I was speaking, the police chief received an emergency call. I was later told that the very school I had mentioned had gone on lockdown due to a possible shooter who was threatening the school!

I don't believe this frightening incident was a *fulfillment* of what I saw in the vision, but I think it served as a *warning sign*. In my private meeting, I told the mayor and the police chief a unique strategy that could hinder and possibly prevent such an attack from taking place.

They both said they had never thought of this idea. It involved forming a group of retired police and military personnel to serve as security inside the school and rotate out each week. Both the police and military are experienced, and many retirees would love to serve in such a capacity.

One of the great lessons my father taught me is that a warning is given, first and foremost, to cause the receiver to pray to perhaps prevent it from happening. At times, people have been warned but never heeded the warning, or they neglected fasting and prayer that could have prevented the problem. It is my hope that prayer, wisdom, and a strategy will form a hedge, and any plots will be exposed and stopped in advance.

When it comes to the plans of terrorists, the Holy Spirit is more than able to reveal even the smallest details, thereby allowing the receiver to provide vital information to proper authorities who can take action to prevent the attacks. Of course, only those who believe in spiritual dreams and visions are willing to listen to these types of warnings. Many secular or non-Christian educators would mock the warnings as a pizza dream.

While the US military was actively looking for Saddam Hussein, I had a strange dream of Saddam in a cave-like setting. Pastor Steve Munsey from Munster, Indiana dreamed he saw Saddam as a little boy, hiding in a hole. Steve called a contact in Washington, DC and suggested going to the places in Iraq where Saddam lived as a young boy. They began a search and found Saddam hiding in a six to eight-foot-deep hole, just nine miles outside of his hometown of Tikrit.

Christ said that the Holy Spirit will show you things to come (John 16:13). Knowing the future is important for knowing and following God's will, and for warnings that could save you from trouble, save your life or someone else's, or prevent a national tragedy.

CHAPTER 13

VISIONS OF CREMATION OVENS

In August of 2021, I was in my office at the Voice of Evangelism ministry center when I experienced a strange and troubling series of visions. Each day, around 1:30 to 2:30, I set aside about an hour to pray. I had turned the lights out and was leaning back in a chair and praying quite intensely. I will pray, then sit still for a few minutes, then pray again, become silent, and repeat the process. I have learned that the Lord cannot speak to my spirit if I'm talking. I can't hear His voice if I am hearing only my voice.

My eyes had been closed for about thirty minutes. Suddenly, I began to see something forming in the darkness. At first, objects appeared a bit blurry, then when I began to focus, I saw clearly. I was fully aware, completely awake but with my eyes closed, and could speak to myself or out loud.

Forming in my vision was some sort of metal wall with a round door. I was uncertain what the object was, but as I continued to look intently, I observed what appeared to be a clock and a timer. Both had the appearance of a digital clock, and the numbers were bright green. The object soon became very clear, to the point that it seemed I could reach out and touch it. All the while I was saying to myself, "What is this? Why does it have a round door, and why it is metal?"

Suddenly the scene changed. I then observed a rectangular piece of paper that looked about three inches high and six inches wide. It was brown parchment, similar to the color of a brown paper bag. There was writing in black ink, with about seven or eight lines of information. I attempted to read the words on this parchment. However, within seconds the background surrounding the letters turned dark, and the parchment slowly began to burn.

This scene changed to a third and different view. Instead of the brown parchment, something that looked like a world map suddenly appeared. It was the same size of the previous piece of paper. However, this map had no color, only black. Every continent was completely black. The United States, Canada, Latin America, all of Europe, every nation was shrouded in blackness. Then I noticed that in many nations there would appear a very tiny pinpoint of light. The light was pure white, but extremely small compared to the darkness in the nation.

The first vision then appeared again. This time the color of the metal was pale green. I saw another digital monitor with a green number 10 on it.

It was then that I perceived this was a cremation oven. I had never seen one, nor had I ever been in a place where cremation was performed. I was uncertain about the two other parts of this vision, although the burning parchment and the dark map were not positive signs in the least.

SEVERAL DAYS LATER

Several days later, on Friday, August 13th, two members of my ministry staff and I were flying to Texas for five weekend services. I was in my normal seat on the plane and was a bit tired. I wanted to rest a while before arriving and ministering that night in Willis, Texas.

I rested but was not asleep. I was mentally alert and fully aware of my surroundings. My eyes were closed. Within moments, three distinct, full color images appeared in succession. Once again, I saw three different types of cremation ovens. The first was a metal oven with a large round metal door. The scene changed. I saw a second oven, which had a square door. That image faded, and I saw the third oven with an arched door. All three were ovens of different types. I saw what appeared to be either a meter or some type of timer attached to the front of each.

Later, when I had access to the internet, I looked up the word "cremation" and clicked onto the images. To my shock, there were several different types of ovens, including one with a circular door. I also identified the other two from the doors I saw from the internet pictures.

The combination of two visions, that close together, indicates something of importance. The visions troubled my spirit for many days. To this day, when recalling these visions, I feel uneasy.

WHAT IS COMING?

In the United States and much of the world, there are two primary ways of caring for bodies of the deceased: the traditional coffin burial and the cremation process. To see three different types of ovens and a map of the world shrouded in black indicates to me that there is coming some type of tragedy that will cause a massive number of deaths—so many that it will be either medically or physically impossible to conduct traditional funerals or burials. I have considered three possibilities.

First is the possibility that a dangerous and deadly pestilence or bioweapon will be released and quickly spread from nation to nation. It would have to cause so many deaths at once that the deceased would be unable to be buried in the traditional manner. The sheer number of deaths would require cremation. We have witnessed how quickly Covid-19 spread globally from nation to nation, eventually shutting down much of the world. For cremation to be the choice of burial, there might also be concerns that the disease would remain on the corpse after death, thus necessitating the use of cremation.

The second possibility could be a natural disaster. For example, a massive earthquake, especially one occurring on a major fault line, with a high magnitude on the Richter scale, would collapse buildings and skyscrapers in cities. On the coast it could trigger a tsunami. These are the type of disasters that could send death rates soaring, depending on the population of the impacted areas. During any earthquake or other tragedy when buildings collapse, it is often days or even weeks before bodies are recovered. If the death toll was massive, it would be nearly impossible to provide a traditional burial for the victims.

A third possibility, and the most extreme and unlikely, could be a strike from a large asteroid. Depending upon the size and the strike zone, many deaths could occur in a concentrated area.

When there are massive numbers of deaths where the bodies remain unburied, eventually disease spreads, with the potential to harm to the living. This could explain why cremation is the choice of burial.

During the second wave of Covid-19, the infection rate rose so fast in India that in one area, over three hundred people died in a twenty-four-hour period. In another city, over seventy bodies were cremated in one day alone. For any nation to cremate large numbers of people would require a calamity of such magnitude that hundreds or thousands of deaths would have to occur in one location at the same time.

This vision could indicate a massive number of deaths in nations where cremation of bodies is common. China cremates a higher number of people than another other country (millions each year), but Japan has the highest rates of cremation—over 99%. Other countries in the Far East have high rates of cremation as well. This method is increasing across the world, and especially in nations and cities that don't have much land for coffin burials.

The most recent time in history that involved cremation ovens and a massive number of deaths was during the Holocaust. According to the Jewish Virtual Library, the Nazis built four crematoria with gas chambers at Auschwitz II-Birkenau. They used gas to kill hundreds of thousands of men, women, and children, then burned their bodies in cremation ovens. According to German authorities, 340 bodies could be burned every 24 hours after installing three of the furnaces.

Years ago, while at the Greenbrier in West Virginia, we toured a bunker that was built to secure federal government leaders in the event of a nuclear attack. The tour guide showed our group a large, iron oven that would be used if people living in the bunker died while it was not possible to bury them outdoors.

As for these visions of cremation ovens, I am uncertain of the areas or the timing of these things. However, I say with certainty that these were clear visions.

Often, when a Christian in America experiences a warning dream or vision, they tend to think the warning or message is just for the United States, but this is not always the case. Lot's warning of destruction was sent to four of five cities clustered in one location, while Noah's warning was global. Christ's prediction of Jerusalem's desolation impacted both Jerusalem and all of Judea (Matt. 24). However, history indicates that in the same year, AD 70, when Jerusalem was in ashes, other surrounding provinces and countries escaped the Roman legions while also surviving the destruction of Jerusalem.

The Jewish historian Josephus recorded the world's first prophetic word, dating back to the time of Adam. According to an ancient oracle God gave to Adam directly, He would allow the world to be destroyed twice: the first time by the volume of water, and the second time by fire. Water is the heavenly sign linked with the days of Noah. Fire is connected with the days of Lot (Luke 17:26-30). We constantly hear of flood and fire disasters sweeping the earth. These are signs of the birth pangs of the Messiah.

I will neither add to nor take away from what I saw in these two visions. We see through a glass darkly and know only in part. However, at some point in times to come, I believe there will be a massive number of cremations somewhere in the world, or perhaps throughout the world.

CHAPTER 14

TSUNAMI WARNINGS FOR THE UNITED STATES

The modern world became acquainted with the destructive power of water when devastating tsunamis struck Indonesia and Japan, killing tens of thousands of innocent and unsuspecting people. Homes and businesses were washed away, and large ships were tossed like plastic toys.

Christ predicted that unusual end-time signs would be seen in the sea:

> *"And there shall be signs in the sun, and in the moon, and in the stars; and upon the earth distress of nations, with perplexity; the sea and the waves roaring."*
>
> – LUKE 21:25 (KJV)

This is the only New Testament reference that reveals strange activity occurring in the sea. The key word is "roaring." This word appears only two times in the English translation of the New Testament; once in Luke and once in 1 Peter 5:8, where Peter compares Satan to a roaring lion.

Two different Greek words are used in these verses. For roaring lion, the word is *oruomai*, which refers to the sound of roaring—that is, the noise made by a lion. The word in Luke 21:25 is *echeo*, from where we derive the English word echo. This roar alludes to a loud noise that comes from the waves and the sea. When a tsunami is approaching the coastline, eyewitnesses often speak of a strange sound, sometimes described as a roar.

A tsunami can occur when there is a sudden displacement of the plates on the ocean floor, caused by movement such as an earthquake. This creates large waves that travel at high speeds and eventually make their way to coastal shorelines. If the waves are high and strong enough, they will crash into buildings, lift homes off their foundations, tumble vehicles and boats, and uproot trees and anything else in their path.

The Red Sea (Heb. 11:29) was a pivotal geographical location in the narrative of the Israelites crossing from Egypt's border toward the Promised Land. The Almighty split open the sea, causing the water to stand as a heap and form massive walls, with a one-way road leading out of Egypt. For the Israelites, their feet remained dry on the path God formed. However, as Pharaoh and the Egyptians drove their chariots into the huge opening, the water walls collapsed, drowning Pharaoh and his military leadership. *That which was a miracle for Israel became judgment on the Egyptian Empire!*

In the Apocalypse, the Apostle John pierced the veil and saw thousands of years into the future, revealing that a star (in Greek, this is an asteroid) will fall from heaven, strike the earth, and burn up a third of the grass and trees. The impact will also pollute the fountains of water. This would be a land strike and not necessarily a strike in the ocean (Rev. 8:10-11). In the same chapter, John wrote:

> *"And the second angel sounded, and as it were a great mountain burning with fire was cast into the sea: and the third part of the sea became blood; And the third part of the creatures which were in the sea, and had life, died; and the third part of the ships were destroyed."evelation 8:8-9 (KJV)*

When studying each Greek word and the imagery John presented, this appears to be a large, inactive volcano on a coastal area, near a major sea, that suddenly becomes violently active. The text does not indicate *where* this cosmic strike will occur, but the vision does reveal the damage caused when this mountain breaks off into the sea. Scientists have pointed out the possibility that, if a mountain that's part of an island broke off into the ocean through an earthquake or volcanic activity, the impact would create a powerful tsunami and send a large, destructive wave across the ocean. This could explain how a third of the ships in the sea will be destroyed. A high tsunami wave could topple any boat or ship in its path.

THE TSUNAMI VISIONS

When I explain the details of a personal vision (or a dream), I like to remind the listener that when these experiences occurred, often in the middle of the night or in the early hour before sunrise, I was not watching a movie or a tsunami documentary, nor was I discussing or thinking about tsunamis before bedtime. In each instance, what I saw was an unexpected encounter that was seared into my mind and spirit.

Up to the time of this writing, none of the tsunamis I have seen have happened. However, as I mentioned previously, there are times that a vision may not be fulfilled for weeks, months, or years. The Lord is longsuffering (patient), giving individuals, cities, and nations the opportunity to repent of personal sins and national iniquities, turn to Him, and seek His mercy. God revealed to Noah, "My Spirit shall not always strive [deal] with man" (Gen. 6:3). There is a set time for the fulfillment of a warning or judgment.

The numerous tsunami warnings that I have been shown began several years ago. There was a season of about six months in which it seemed that every few weeks, I was having tsunami dreams. While the majority were dreams, at least three were visions. The clarity, the alert senses, and the fact that the troubling images remained with me all indicated that these dreams and visions were supernatural manifestations and warnings for the United States.

The tsunamis originated from the three possible areas in the US: the East Coast, the West Coast, and the Gulf of Mexico. I do not believe these all happened at the same time or were the same tsunami, but were three different locations during three different time frames.

THE COAST OF SOUTH CAROLINA

This vision was very detailed. I was with my wife and several of her family members. It was as though we were on some type of family gathering or vacation. We were staying on an upper floor of a building, looking out the window into a city next to the ocean. The buildings were not crowded skyscrapers such as you would see in a place like New York City, but were business offices with glass fronts located near where we were staying.

I looked out the large window and saw a black tornado beginning to form in the atmosphere above the buildings downtown. I knew that a bad storm was about to hit. Outside on the sidewalk was a woman taking pictures. I tapped on the window to get her attention and yelled for her to get to safety. Turning to my right, looking out another large glass window, I saw a view of the ocean. In the distance was a large bridge connecting two sections of land. At that moment, two things occurred simultaneously.

First, a large tsunami wave began to form in the distance, out in the ocean. It was high enough to cover the two-story building we were in. The size reminded me of waves you see at the professional surfing competitions in Hawaii. However, this was not a normal wave; it was destructive.

On the bridge I noticed a large green sign, such as the ones posted along an interstate that show the names of towns or highway exits ahead. The sign I saw clearly read *Charleston*. I knew that if a person crossed the bridge, it would lead them to Charleston, South Carolina. As the massive wave prepared to crash into the coastal city, the bridge began to shake. At that moment, I saw a final harbinger.

Rising from the water was a ghostly form of the World Trade Center Towers that collapsed in 2001. The shadowy images rose above the wave on the ocean side where the bridge was located. The bridge began to collapse into the water. As it did, I heard the wave hit the side of the building we were in. Everything began to shake violently.

I suddenly came out of the vision and found myself shaking in the dark bedroom. It was impossible to go back to sleep, so I got up and wrote down what I had seen. Details have remained with me to this day.

BALTIMORE AND THE MARYLAND COAST

A few years ago, I experienced three different visions over a timeframe of about one year. The first was of a sudden tsunami that occurred outside of Baltimore, Maryland. The city of Baltimore sits on a harbor and a river that feed into the Chesapeake Bay. It seems that it would be impossible to see the amount of water I saw coming in from the bay area. However, on July 8, 2020 at 11:30 pm, a report came across the news indicating that a rare tsunami had formed in the Chesapeake Bay during a series of storms. It was called a meteotsunami, the type that can form in bays and over lakes when conditions are right during serious and dangerous winds and storms.

For about sixteen consecutive years, Pam and I ministered at a church in Edgemere, Maryland, a quaint town just off the water about twenty-five miles from Baltimore. In the first vision, I was in a home in

Edgemere, the one where my wife and I stayed during our early years of ministry at this church. In the vision, I was outside in the front yard when water suddenly began pouring into the streets and covering the yard. I yelled, "It's a tsunami! Get inside and get upstairs now!" As I made my way upstairs, I grabbed as much food and bottled water as I could carry. With my arms full, I ran to the second floor of the house. I looked behind me and saw that water was swiftly coming through the doors and filling up the first floor. I never saw how high the water rose in the home, but I knew this was becoming a very dangerous situation.

Sometime thereafter, a second night vision unfolded. I was in the same home, but this time I was inside looking at a different view when the water came rushing in. I was filling up bathtubs and sinks with water, knowing that this event could damage water pipes and limit fresh water. As I hastily filled the tubs and sinks, I told someone behind me (I did not see who it was) that water would be precious in coming days, and not to unplug the tubs but to use the water for drinking water. I seemed to know that storing water in tubs and sinks would be helpful.

The third vision was similar to the other visions. I knew it was the same region of the country, and a tsunami was forming. The homes and buildings would be in danger. The emphasis in the third vision seemed to be on the need to have non-perishable foods that would last for many days. In this vision, I was moving quickly in the kitchen to grab and fill a bag with as much food as possible. Water was overtaking the first floor, and those with me were swiftly moving to rooms on the second floor.

I do not believe these were three separate events. I believe it was the same event from three different perspectives. The first was the warning of what was coming. The second emphasized the need for fresh water, while the third revealed the need to have supplies of food for an extended period. In all three of these, the tsunami was coming from the Chesapeake Bay. It could be possible that the tsunami in South Carolina and the one in Maryland are from the same tsunami.

PANIC FOLLOWS

When Hurricane Katrina struck New Orleans, the excessive amount of water caused the levies to break, flooding and destroying entire neighborhoods. Live news reports shocked the nation as we saw water as high as the gutters on homes and people on their roofs, frantically waving their arms to be rescued. Some fled into their attics, where they were trapped. Many perished.

When coronavirus lockdowns were forced upon cities and entire states, people were instructed to remain inside their dwellings for fourteen days. Many offices were closed for months, with employees forced to work from home. One news report from New York showed people standing in long lines, wearing masks, and purchasing food. News channels soon reported that workers connected with food processing plants, suppliers, and grocery stores were catching the virus, causing a vital shortage of labor. This also included food harvesters at US farms. Fear and panic sent millions of people into grocery stores, filling their carts with more than they needed, causing shortages of many items.

I live in Bradley County in Southeast Tennessee, with a population of just over 110,000. For several months, the grocery store shelves were completely empty of certain items. Within an hour of restocking shelves, they again would be empty of certain products. It was a visible example of what can happen when panic sets in.

THE HAWAII TSUNAMI

I have traveled to and ministered in Hawaii, one of the most beautiful American states with kind and hospitable people. But natural disasters pay no attention to the beauty of a place or the wonderful people who live there. The fact is the earth is convulsing in what the prophetic scriptures call birth pangs (Matt. 24:8 – *sorrows* is the word used in the KJV). These pains include natural disasters—earthquakes, hurricanes, tornados, floods, volcanic eruptions, and tsunamis. Christ taught that it rains on the just and the unjust (Matt. 5:45). This verse indicates that rain (figuratively speaking, storms) falls on all people, both good and bad, just and unjust.

A more recent vivid night vision involved what appeared to be an area in Hawaii. Eight main islands make up the state of Hawaii, although the state recognizes a total of 137 islands that make up the Hawaiian Island chain. Through the years, when undersea earthquakes have occurred off the coast of places such as Japan or California, Hawaii has received warnings to alert the islanders to the possibility of a tsunami.

In this detailed and troubling vision, I was standing at a beach near the ocean, which could be anywhere, except the beach was at the base of massive fern and forest-covered rocks similar to the types I have seen in Hawaii. In the vision, I knew it was somewhere in Hawaii. The beach was crowded with people of all ages, many sitting on chairs and towels while children were playing in the sand. In the distance, I observed large waves and surfers riding the waves to shore. The sky was clear, and everyone was enjoying their day.

Suddenly I was caught up in the atmosphere. Looking down, I saw details and activities for a long distance. I heard a rumbling noise from the ocean and felt a strong shaking. I could see a large tsunami wave forming. I knew it would strike the area and everyone was in danger. I began to yell, "Get out! Run! A tsunami is coming!" I kept yelling my warning. However, the people appeared distracted or unconcerned. A few took notice and began grabbing children and running toward several buildings on shore.

I did not see the tsunami when it finally hit the shoreline, as the scene changed to the aftermath. There were so many bodies lying in different places. The most shocking scenes were several people who had been buried under the sand, and I could see hands, arms, legs, and feet protruding from piles of sand on the beach. Survivors were gathered in various buildings, and some homes built on higher ground became shelters for survivors.

THE COAST OF CALIFORNIA

One of my favorite places to minister in the United States is in California at Free Chapel in Orange County. The people in attendance are spiritually hungry for biblical truth, and some are intense prayer warriors. Despite our impressions of California as a center of worldliness and debauchery, there are many areas in the state where revival is beginning to break out.

In this strange dream, which again was more like a vision, Pastor Jentezen Franklin and I were passengers on a private plane flying out of John Wayne Airport in Orange County, not far from the church. The airport is about fifteen miles from Laguna Beach along the Pacific coastline.

Our plane was on the runway. The pilot was revving up the engines. I could feel the thrust from the takeoff. This is when I looked out the window, just in time to see a massive tsunami wave that had formed in the ocean. Of all the dreams and visions, this was undoubtedly the highest wave I had seen. It looked to be a hundred feet high. I was yelling to the pilot, "Get higher, get higher!" At this point, I awoke, unable to return to sleep.

Months later, a second night vision unfolded when I was in a deep sleep. This again was more of a vision than a dream. The images were sharp and clear, as if I were physically in the location.

This was the same event from a different perspective. I was once again in Southern California, riding in an SUV with my wife and a few ministry team members. We were driving up a mountain when suddenly rivers of water began pouring in from the coast, filling up the ravines and canyons around this mountain. We sped up the mountain away from the water, where we located a nice home built near the top of the mountain. We left the vehicle and someone in our group knocked on the door. A well-dressed elderly woman answered the door. She immediately recognized me from our weekly television program and invited our group inside. She had a satellite news feed on her television. Fox News was already reporting that a strong earthquake in the Pacific had created a massive tsunami on the coast of California. There were live news feeds coming in from helicopters flying over areas where water had covered homes and buildings. I recall seeing fast moving water take down everything in its path.

This tsunami produced a massive wave that appeared to be as high as a hundred feet. Because the woman's home was at the top of a mountain, she was not directly impacted by the water that had poured in and made its way into the cities.

It is possible the California and Hawaii tsunamis are connected. However, those in Hawaii would be warned hours in advance, giving time to clear the beaches and low-lying areas and head to safety. In the vision, however, only a few heeded the warning.

SHOULD YOU STAY?

One reason I am hesitant to speak about these types of visions is that people often respond by asking me questions I am unable to answer. The common question is, "I live in (or close to) one of these areas. Should I move my family now to another location?" Here is my answer.

These types of warnings are often given months, years, or decades in advance to offer people in the target zone the opportunity to fast, pray, repent, and possibly hold back the hand of destruction. The city of Jerusalem continued to exist for nearly forty years before Christ's warning of destruction and desolation came to pass.

Josephus wrote that one man began attending festivals at the temple in Jerusalem, and for six years he continually cried out warnings against the sins of the city. When the day came that his six years of warnings were fulfilled, a stone from a Roman catapult struck him in the head and killed him. The warnings came first, extended mercy was sent, and the destruction finally came.

Each person should fast and pray and seek God for His direction. When Lot chose where to live, he picked the Valley of Siddim, the location of the city of Sodom. This was one of the largest cities in Canaan (Gen. 14). Abraham was living about sixty miles away in Beersheba. The two places are examples of contrast. Sodom was wicked, Beersheba was not. Sodom was engulfed in sexual perversion, Beersheba was not. Sodom was a dangerous place at night, Beersheba was not.

From Beersheba, Abraham could see the smoke ascending, as the smoke of a furnace, when Sodom was burning. Sodom was wiped out, while Beersheba experienced no smoke or flames. Beersheba, a community in the Negev Desert built around seven wells of water, was unaffected.

Genesis 14 lists five cities located in the plains. When the fire and brimstone fell, four of the five cities were consumed to ashes. The fifth, a small community named Zoar that was built on a mountain, was spared from the fire. Here again, four cities were exceedingly wicked, and one was not. There are towns and cities within the United States where there is less iniquity, and others that are filled with every possible sin. Some states elect radical leftist politicians, while others elect more sensible leaders with morals and integrity. Leaders can make or break a city, state, or nation.

The bottom line is, only you know where you and your family should live. Families must pray and carefully discern the geographical area in which they are to live and raise their families. With these visions, I did not receive any indication of the timeframe in which the events could happen. Lot made his move away from Sodom a few hours before the fire fell. If you relocate, you may be given a long time to prepare, or as Lot, your move may be days or hours before the fire falls. Be sensitive to the Holy Spirit and listen for instructions. Remember what Peter said about Lot: "The Lord knows how to deliver the godly out of temptations, and to reserve the unjust unto the day of judgment to be punished" (2 Pet. 2:9).

CHAPTER 15

NUCLEAR POWER PLANTS AND A STOCK MARKET COLLAPSE

These unusual visions have not yet transpired, to my knowledge. I believe this vivid and detailed vision refers to an attack on one or more nuclear facilities and the impact upon the stock market in the United States.

The vision began with my wife, our children, and me inside a house. This was not the home Pam and I live in now, nor a home that we have owned in the past. It was a nice, one-level home such as you could find in any middle-class neighborhood.

Suddenly I heard my son Jonathan yell out, "Dad, come and see this!" I ran to the side door of this house and looked out at a large and flat open field. To my left I could see in the distance a large nuclear cooling tower, such as the type seen at any nuclear power plant. I eventually saw two towers a short distance apart. In the far distance were three other towers, for a total of five.

The closest tower on the left began to spin, taking on the form of a massive tornado. The reaction from the first tower set in motion a spinning reaction at the second nuclear tower, positioned not far from the first. One tower was located along a coastal area near water, and the other was nearby, but on land. Near the tower, I saw two very tall trees, both of which appeared dead and as though they were bleached white. Neither tree had leaves or fruit on them.

I turned to the field and saw a strange sight to the right. Stampeding at full speed were hundreds of bulls, all with long horns, running from the far end of the field toward the house. I noticed they all had hides that were white with large black spots. I saw Pam running in the field toward me. I yelled to her, "Quick, get the kids and get into the basement!"

These bulls were in panic mode, all running in the same direction. It was a frightening, violent stampede. I knew they were reacting to the disaster involving the two nuclear towers. I then awoke and immediately went into my home office to write down every detail.

When interpreting this vision, there are numerous interesting points, including the symbolism. First, the home represented the average American home, as this was not my home, nor was it one I was familiar with. It seemed that what was occurring would impact the average family in some way. I think the two nuclear cooling towers represented nuclear power plants. The nuclear power plants that I have seen always have at least two cooling towers, or stacks. These towers are used to remove heat from the circulating water before it is returned to its source. The spinning towers indicate trouble (a storm) coming that is a result of some disaster at the nuclear plant.

The two trees can have two meanings. In the Bible, King Nebuchadnezzar was given a troubling dream of a large, fruitful tree being cut down, leaving only the stump in the earth. In Daniel's interpretation, the tree represented the king himself, whom God was going to remove (cut down) from his position as king. These two trees could represent two leaders or people who will be directly impacted by what occurs. The lack of leaves or fruit indicated death of some type. Of course, it could also allude to radiation leakage causing death to the environment, or deaths caused by what occurred at the two towers.

In Christ's parables, the field represents the world (Matt. 13:38). I knew in the vision that the bulls represented the US stock market. When the market is high or going up, it is called a bull market. With seeing nothing but bulls, this event seems likely to transpire when the stock market is doing well. The sudden and unexpected crisis immediately sends the bulls running in the opposite direction, seemingly out of fear. Thus, the running bulls could refer to a possible crash of the stock market.

A stock market correction is when the market falls ten to twenty percent from its 52-week high. Corrections are not uncommon. A crash is a sudden and dramatic drop in stock prices that results in a significant loss of wealth on paper. Crashes are often driven by panic selling after a significant event. A correction happens over a period of time, while a crash can occur overnight and have a devastating effect on consumer confidence.

I was intrigued by the appearance of the bulls. The cows with white hair and large black spots are Holsteins. The Holstein originated in Europe over 2,000 years ago. This breed has the highest milk production in the world and can be found on every continent. The cow's one weakness is that they have little resistance to heat diseases when they are in a difficult agro-ecological area.

Since these are important cattle for meat and milk production, the added symbolism may indicate damage to the farm or milk industry, connected to whatever occurs with the two cooling towers.

IS THIS POSSIBLE?

When I had this vision, there was much political discussion concerning Iran's nuclear ambitions, especially since most Iranian Islamic clerics and leaders tend to be anti-Israel and anti-America. Iran has a nuclear program, and they are enriching uranium that they claim will be used for nuclear energy.

Israeli intelligence believes the main goal of Iran's uranium enrichment program is to build nuclear bombs so they can join other nations with a nuclear arsenal. For years, Israeli military leaders have been discussing a precision strike against the nuclear facilities in Iran. Nuclear weapons in Iran's possession would change the entire face of the Persian Gulf and the Middle East.

In light of this possibility, a few years ago I was in a deep sleep and suddenly found myself in the atmosphere over a nation, looking down on their nuclear cooling towers. Suddenly, a strange missile exploded over the area, creating a bluish streak of fire, almost like lightning. It released an energy that hit what appeared to be the fuel storage units in surrounding areas. I heard someone behind me say, "That is a small EMP from the Israelis, sent to disable the computers in this area."

I later asked a former member of the military what it looks like when an EMP is detonated. I saw three unclassified pictures, much like computer-generated color images, of a small test that had been conducted. It looked like the streaks I saw in the vision.

Time will tell, but it may be possible for Israel or her allies to assist in taking out the nuclear program of Iran or some other rogue nation by using this type of weapon to prevent the activation of computer systems that control missiles. I am not a military expert, so this is only speculation based on limited knowledge and information.

The Israeli Defense Force and former Prime Minister Benjamin Netanyahu are set against the Iranians having any type of nuclear weapon. The Iranian leaders are Shi'ite Muslims, while much of the Gulf are Sunni Muslims. The two groups have internally battled for centuries over which group is the true heir of Mohammad. They both believe in the Koran and the Hadith but have differing opinions and traditions.

On multiple occasions, Iran has accused Israel and the United States of hacking into their military facilities and infecting their computers with viruses. In 2020, Iran blamed Israel for an attack on the Natanz nuclear enrichment facility, which took place hours after officials at the reactor started spinning centrifuges that speed up the production of enriched uranium.

Mossad, Israel's intelligence agency, was accused of playing a key role in the attack. Israel was also blamed for killing Iran's chief nuclear scientist. Stuxnet was a complex malware cyber weapon that damaged Iran's nuclear program from 2007 to 2010, causing enough problems to set back their program for an estimated two years. There have been discussions for several years about the possibility of an Israeli air strike against Iran's nuclear facilities, including underground bases called missile cities that Iran claims to have.

NUCLEAR ENERGY

Nuclear power plants provide electricity to entire cities, as the nations have relied more and more on nuclear energy. Many are concerned about the stability of the power grid in the United States, and we know the challenges we would face from power outages if they occurred in extremely cold or hot months of the year.

In this vision, when the towers began to spin, they resembled a tornado. In dreams and visions, a tornado is not always a literal one, but it can represent a severe crisis, especially for people who live in the affected areas.

Any attack or incident involving a nuclear energy plant or the power grid—whether through a weather disaster, a terrorist attack, or any other possible cause—could bring trouble for days, weeks, or even months. Without electricity, everything comes to a halt. Computers, cell phones, and anything that runs on rechargeable batteries would stop functioning. There would be no form of communication that requires electricity, no working pumps at the gas station, no lights on at night, and so on. Any serious disruption certainly would impact cities, municipalities, businesses, the stock market, and the supply chain.

This vision shows an event that could occur at some point in the future. In summary, it will involve at least one nuclear power plant with two cooling towers, or two different nuclear plants represented by two different towers. Whatever happens could cause the demise of two leaders, or the bleached trees could represent a terrible eco-crisis for plant life in the region. The event will likely occur when the stock market is bullish, or at a high point. When news reaches the public, great fear and panic will spread in parts of the world, represented by the field (Matt. 13:38), and will immediately cause people to sell stocks, represented by hundreds of bulls running together as a stampede across the field.

Various things must be considered when people plan for how they would deal with a power blackout. For example, try in advance to find other sources of energy for boiling water and cooking food. Purchase small solar devices that charge a phone. Consider purchasing indoor and outdoor solar powered lightbulbs for emergency power outages.

Proverbs 22:3 says it well: "A prudent man foresees evil and hides himself, but the simple pass on and are punished."

CHAPTER 16

AN EARTHQUAKE IN ST. LOUIS

For several consecutive years, our ministry conducted an annual regional conference in the St. Louis, Missouri area, hosted at Life Church by a dear and close friend, Pastor Rick Shelton. We also ministered at Twin Rivers, where Dr. Bryan Cutshall, another dear friend, served as pastor. Pam and I, along with our ministry team, enjoyed being with the wonderful people at each location. (As a side note, we enjoyed eating lunch at the famous Pasta House.)

Prior to one trip, I experienced two vivid visions that involved the St. Louis area. In this first vision, several members of my travel ministry team and I were hosting a Voice of Evangelism conference at a church in St. Louis. In the vision, I was staying at a local hotel with the team. I later wrote down the names of each team member present in the vision. The team members that I saw still join us to this day, assisting at our ministry resource tables.

The first scene began with me standing in my hotel room, when suddenly the room began to shake violently. I immediately knew I was in the middle of a very strong earthquake. I yelled to Pam, "Go right now and start filling up the sink and bathtub with water, before the water pipes break!" I knew the water pipes, and thus fresh water, would be affected by this earthquake. By the time Pam got to the bathroom, it was too late. The clear, clean water that should have been coming out was brown, having already been mixed with dirt.

We ended up with our team outside the hotel. I saw our book-keeper Susan, and Pat and Carl Craig, a precious couple who still attend conferences and occasionally travel with our volunteer team. Although it wasn't necessary to tell them, I said, "We have just experienced an earthquake. There will be aftershocks, so be ready."

The scene changed and I was standing on a street near grocery stores and some type of outdoor market. Large numbers of people were running into the stores, piling items into carts and carrying as much food and bottled water as possible. Because of the panic in this large city and the possibility of violence due to a lack of supplies, I knew it was important for our group *not to separate*, but to stay together.

Exactly one year later, this vision was followed by a two-part dream of an earthquake. In the first part, the ministry team was in a building when the facility began to shake violently. I could see the walls moving. There were other people in the building as well, and all of us were attempting to stay together and find a safe place away from those who were in a total panic. When an event like this occurs, even good and decent people panic, and all restraints are removed. Looting and robbery become more common.

As I stood outside, I looked around and could see a black tornado forming in the distance. It moved speedily toward something that appeared to be a radio-television tower. This tower was important for communication and was about to take a direct hit from this powerful black tornado. The tornado is symbolic of a dire situation, or a dangerous and destructive event (storm), and this tower could symbolize that communication systems could be cut off due to the quake. I told my team members to get into a big and sturdy concrete basement nearby. They were taking food and water with them, some of which we carry with us in our vehicles to our larger conferences.

We each were aware that this storm would impact much in this area. We, along with others, made our way into a basement (which might have been a storm shelter). It became a bit crowded, and we knew because of road damage that we could be in this location for a while.

THE NEW MADRID FAULT LINE

With the first vision of the earthquake being in St. Louis, I was aware that the New Madrid Fault Line runs through this part of the United States. Say the word earthquake, and the West Coast immediately comes to mind. Americans have been concerned for decades about the possibility of "the Big One" along California's San Andreas Fault Line, but people tend to forget about the major fault line that runs 120 miles down the middle of the country. If a high magnitude earthquake were to occur here, it could potentially affect parts of eight states—Illinois, Indiana, Missouri, Arkansas, Kentucky, Tennessee, Oklahoma, and Mississippi. The last time a large magnitude earthquake occurred on this fault line was in the 1800s. There were no massive causalities at that time, mostly since the affected areas were not heavily populated. Damage did occur in Cincinnati and St. Louis, and the quake was felt as far away as Connecticut.

The earthquakes in the 1800s did cause geological land changes in several states, however. Some places around the fault line have sand-blows, which are areas where water shoots through soil and erupts at the surface. Such liquefaction causes unstable ground, and the level of destruction would depend on the magnitude of the quake and the amount of water saturation.

One of my dear friends, Pastor John Kilpatrick, leader of the historic Brownsville Revival in Pensacola, Florida, has shared a dream he had in 2008. He dreamed of being suspended over a river. Suddenly it vanished, and he was taken up into a school building that began to shake so violently that his teeth were shaking in the dream. As the dream ended, he saw two words that appeared on an old parchment: Indianola and Europa. When he awoke, he was still shaking. After looking up both words, he discovered that both are towns that still exist today, and both are on the New Madrid Fault Line.

One of America's worst earthquakes occurred in 1906 in San Francisco, California. It ignited fires that burned for three days, destroyed nearly five hundred city blocks, and killed an estimated three thousand people. Great anxiety and fear spread throughout the West Coast, and Los Angeles was warned that the city might be in danger. That same month in 1906, a great revival known as the Azusa Street Revival broke out in Los Angeles. It continued for seven years and impacted the lives of tens of thousands of attendees.

Carnal and unbelieving men and women often view the God of the Christians as an angry old deity, full of wrath, with a rod of judgment in one hand and lighting bolts in the other, seeking those whom He may devour. The truth is, God loves the world and does not desire that anyone be lost for eternity. Any selective or national calamity is designed to turn hardhearted men and women to a heart of repentance. Tragic events often bring people to salvation. Our life on earth is like a grain of sand, but eternity is forever. That is where we need to keep our focus.

CHAPTER 17

VISION OF A BIO-WEAPON ATTACK ON LONDON

This is only the second time in years that I have shared this vision publicly. While I was searching through my personal journal of dreams and visions, I came across it and was quickened in my spirit to share this here. I do this for believers to begin to intercede so that hopefully our prayers can expose any terrorists' plots and the right people will be able to stop what could occur.

This vision took place at 3:30 in the morning on April 7 (I did not record the year) while my wife and I were visiting her sister in Northport, Alabama. The vision was vivid and detailed, and it occurred while I was in a deep sleep. I had been dreaming, but suddenly found myself in a situation that was so realistic it was as though it were occurring in real time.

I was walking in what appeared to be a military base with numerous men in uniform. They were in a plane hangar and seemed to be studying detailed plans for an upcoming military exercise.

I approached one man and asked him if he knew of a particular Colonel who worked in counterterrorism in a certain city in America. I looked for his card and phone number, which at the time I carried in my wallet. In the vision I was unable to find it.

In the vision I began to tell the man the details of how I saw the future 9-11 attacks five years before they occurred. Suddenly the scene changed, and I was standing inside a large military hanger that would hold planes, but there was corn growing inside. Looking around, it reminded me of the corn I saw in the vision of the World Trade Center attack. However, in this vision the corn inside the large hanger was not green, but the entire field was dried and withered, as though a severe drought or some pestilence had destroyed the crops.

In the 9-11 vision, in front of me at the end of the field stood the World Trade Center building shrouded in black. In this vision, at the end of this dried cornfield stood a landmark I had seen in London, England. It was Big Ben, the famous clock tower at the northern end of the Palace of Westminster. The clock tower was not made of stone as it is today, but of wood; yet the tower and the clock were identical to Big Ben in London. I knew that what I was about to see would occur in London, England.

As I continued to explain the events of the 9-11 vision to the military men, including the story of how I saw five grey tornadoes spinning from the front and sides of a World Trade Center building, I began walking from left to right between the brown cornstalks. I eventually came to the end of the field near the clock tower, where there was another group of soldiers. One mentioned the name Bill Frisk to me. After the vision, I researched and discovered he was a United States senator and a doctor who had studied and was familiar with bio-chemical terrorism.

When I turned behind me, I was then standing in a laundry room where a soldier was pulling his clothes out of one of the machines. When he opened the door to his right, a white watery substance began pouring through the door. Soon, the strange white substance was pouring across the entire floor.

That scene changed. I was standing outside and saw rolling hills and a road. A car approached carrying the driver and a man who was helping us to get out of the area. I grabbed a man beside me and hollered, "Get out of here!"

The vision shifted to a new scene. This time there were rolling hills and valleys, reminding me of a countryside outside of a city. I sensed that we were driving many miles away from London. I told the man with me, "You must learn to fly." I knew this was not referring to flying a plane, but it was a figure of speech for learning to rise above the events—to rise emotionally, mentally, and spiritually higher than your circumstances.

The man who was traveling with me stood beside me on top of a mountain where we looked for miles and realized that terrible destruction had come to the area. Near us I saw a woman pick up a child and say, "You must not stay within ten miles (I assume she was referring to the city of London), or you will be in great danger!" Upon hearing this, I grabbed the man's arm beside me and said, "Fly by faith," meaning, get above this situation.

After saying this, I was physically lifted into the air. In the distance, I could see the white foam flowing on the ground across the hills. As this strange and dangerous substance drew closer, I spoke again to the man with me, explaining that in my 1996 vision of New York City's terrorist attack, I saw people running into churches for prayer and protection. The vision suddenly ended.

A BIOLOGICAL ATTACK?

Notice the parallels: the cornfield—one green and one dry, and the two noted buildings—the World Trade Center tower and the Big Ben clock tower. Both structures were towering at the end of the cornfields. Both visions reveal a warning of some type of attack. The strange white substance could be some type of biological weapon that is so dangerous, people must be ten miles from it to prevent danger or even death. Big

Ben is a British icon located in the political and economic center of the United Kingdom, while New York City is considered the economic and financial center for the United States and much of the world.

British political leaders and their military have been allies with the United States, including during both world wars and in the fight against Islamic fanaticism. Since the mid-1990s, however, many have referred to the city of London as "Londonistan" due to the large and growing population of Muslims in the city. A recent census shows that there are over a million Muslims in greater London, and some have labeled the city a haven for radical Islamists and recruiters. The Muslim population throughout the United Kingdom is over 2.5 million. As of this writing, London's mayor is a devout Muslim. This makes all of England an easy target for radical Islamic terrorists, whose ideology of forced sharia law dramatically differs from that of the West, as well as that of moderate Muslims who support democracy.

One of the concerns of American and British intelligence is that terrorists have observed the impact that *one virus* had on shutting down the entire world's economy. Some counterterrorism experts believe that radical elements are watching from afar, taking notes, and realizing that instead of blowing up cars and buildings, the release of a dangerous and deadly toxin creates more fear, emotional damage, division, and death than cars with explosives or hijacked planes full of passengers.

This is difficult to say, but because this vision was parallel to America's 9-11 terrorist attacks, I believe it could be a warning to London, England of some type of biological or chemical attack in the future.

While preparing this chapter, I came across a note I had stored in a file on my computer. It stated that on a Friday, July 14, I had spoken with a woman who worked as a chemical and biological first responder. At that time (a few years back) a group of specialists had been meeting for several weeks to discuss emergency preparations in the event of a chemical or biological attack. Oddly, she indicated that there are places that appear to be dairy farms, which are not actually dairy farms, but in fact are underground research facilities. She said that some are owned by foreign countries. She had heard me talk about this dangerous, milky-white substance in the vision. She said that something of this nature already exists, and it looks like milk.

I take each of these visions seriously. When I sense a strange heaviness in my spirit (in other words, a burden), I find a place to be alone and pray. We may never know, at least in this life, what disasters our prayers have prevented!

WHAT'S NEXT?

CHAPTER 18

AMERICA'S NORTH AND SOUTH DIVISION

Solomon taught that, what has been is what will be, and there is nothing new under the sun (Eccl. 1:9-10). For years I have taught that history is cyclical, and eventually history repeats itself. The world's prophetic future is concealed in past historical events, biblical stories (especially from the Old Testament), and of course, biblical prophecies that reveal events that will transpire at the time of the end.

The past can be concealed in the future, as cyclical patterns repeat themselves with such accuracy that, at the *end* of the historical or biblical narrative, you often discover that the same conclusion *repeated itself.* This is one reason historians are now paying close attention to the causes of the collapse of the Roman Empire. For a while, America has been following the same political, economic, and spiritual trail that eventually led to the demise of the Roman Empire's economic strength, military power, and political influence.

THE AMERICA—ISRAEL LINK

Ancient Israel was one nation with twelve tribal land grants, each with its own land borders. The tribe of Joseph, divided between his two sons, Ephraim and Manasseh, created thirteen tribes. America once was divided into thirteen colonies. The first maps that were drawn show that the borders of the thirteen colonies were similar in shape to the maps of Israel's thirteen tribal borders.

After King Solomon's death, Israel was divided between the *northern* and *southern* kingdoms. The northern tribes eventually turned from the true God, accepted all different religious beliefs, and disobeyed God's law in the Torah. The southern kingdom, consisting of the tribes of Judah and Benjamin, retained the land grant with Jerusalem, the location of the sacred temple. They remained loyal to the rules and statutes of God for many years.

However, foreign nations brought with them their idol gods. Over time, their lifestyle of spiritual darkness and their lack of moral rules corrupted the faith of Israelites in the southern kingdom.

The United States of America was one nation, one Republic that grew from the time we established our three national documents—the Constitution, Declaration of Independence, and Bill of Rights. All three were formed and signed by men of faith, many of whom attended church and considered themselves Christians. Even our Ivy League universities such as Harvard, Yale, Dartmouth, and Princeton were established to train ministers of the gospel.

By the start of the Civil War in 1861, eleven states seceded from the union and eventually formed the Confederate States of America. Those states were South Carolina, Mississippi, Florida, Alabama, Georgia, Louisiana, Texas, Virginia, Arkansas, Tennessee, and North Carolina. They created their own Constitution, known as the Confederate Constitution, which stressed the autonomy of each state.

After the war, the cultural, moral, judicial, and spiritual climate in the Northeast began to change. Today the Northeast (and the North in general) is considered far more liberal than the Southeast (and the South in general). Lists that identify the ten most liberal and conservative states in the United States show us that this trend still holds true.

The most liberal states in the Northeast are:

- Massachusetts is #1

- Maine is #2

- Vermont is #3

- New York is #5

- New Hampshire is #6

- Maryland is #9

By comparison, notice where some of America's conservative states are located:

- Mississippi is #1

- Alabama is #3

- West Virginia is #4

- Tennessee is #6

- Louisiana is #8

- Arkansas is #9

- South Carolina is #10

Depending on the source of the information, the numerical positions of these states can vary, but the same states remain on each list. The biblically, socially, and politically conservative men and women are found predominately in the Southeastern states. Some states labeled as liberal (such as California, Washington, and Oregon) have a conservative population, but it is typically concentrated outside of the large cities, or in certain areas of the state. Southwestern Virginia, Southern Ohio, South Georgia, and Southern Missouri come to mind.

In Israel, the temple was in Judea, in the southern part of the nation where the seven festivals were kept each year. There was a Levitical priesthood and a sacrificial order, and the Torah was being read. As long as the people prayed, worshipped God, and kept the Sabbaths, New Moons, and seven festivals, they retained God's divine favor and blessing.

Eventually, the pagans living among them began to influence the belief system of the southern tribes. Little by little, they started to compromise. The Jews living in Jerusalem and Judea even began to offer their children to the fires of the idol Molech (symbolic of modern-day abortion). In the Torah, God called this act of "passing children through the fire" an abomination. He promised severe judgment on the cities as a penalty for the premeditated slaying of a man and for the shedding of innocent blood (Lev. 18:21; Deut. 19:10 and 21:1-9).

When the righteous began to compromise in small things, larger compromises soon followed. A time came when groups of men who were committing sodomy (an abomination according to Lev. 20:13) set up their camps in tents just outside the temple doors in Jerusalem. As immorality prevailed, these men who committed the same sins that destroyed cities in Lot's generation built personal houses near the temple. God called their acts sin and promised punishment, but the people were ignorant and accepted what God rejected.

God raised up a young king, Josiah, who read the Torah and responded by breaking down the houses of these men and removing them from the city (2 Kings 23:7).

It's possible these Sodomites were deceived in the same manner of some today. Perhaps they believed God changed His mind about sin, since the Torah was an "outdated old manuscript from a past time." Israel had progressed to a new level of tolerance. They lived near the temple in their sins, yet thought they were accepted in God's sight. This is like many people today who live in some form of iniquity, yet attempt to mix the good with the bad. They "mingle the seed" to create a new formula of acceptance under the banner of their progressive tolerance.

America also is divided between a more liberal North and a more conservative South. Just as in Israel, the South is beginning to change, particularly because those from liberal states are moving to conservative states to escape what they created, yet some are bringing that same destructive political, moral, and social ideology with them. Their ideology clashes with the conservative southern ideals that we who are older in faith have held onto firmly. Our universities are also graduating students who develop a leftist and secular worldview, even among those who were raised in church.

CHRISTIANS LIVING IN A PARTY MODE

Christ compared the days of His return to events and conditions occurring in the days of Noah prior to the flood, and during the time of Lot before the destruction of the four cities by fire. However, I want to look at something strange that followed the flood of Noah's day and the destructive fire in Lot's time.

Noah took a hundred years to build the ark. After entering it and shutting the door, he and his family were locked inside the floating zoo for over one year. Noah planted a vineyard after he left the ark, then made wine and drank it. His son Ham, the father of Canaan, found him naked in his tent and told his two brothers. Shem and Japheth walked backwards and covered their father with a garment. Scripture says that when Noah awoke, he knew what his younger son had done. He placed a curse upon Canaan, the youngest son of Ham (Gen. 9:20-25). Without going into great detail, some scholars believe that Canaan may have performed a particular sex act while his grandfather was drunk. This is why the two sons covered him. It is interesting that Canaan was the father of the Canaanites, including the men who eventually became the men of Sodom.

The entire event recorded in Genesis 9 was rooted in one circumstance: Noah was drunk with his homemade wine. Let me say, read the Bible carefully, and you will find that nothing good ever came from a person partaking in alcoholic beverages. Often people become drunk and uninhibited, and their clothes end up coming off. Noah and Lot demonstrate this.

THE REMNANT MUST RISE UP

There is a strong biblical principle of a remnant that rises above the confusion of national chaos. The remnant is not the leftovers, or a small group of people barely surviving a situation, barely holding on, afflicted with weakness, or on the verge of going under. They are not self-appointed chosen ones who perceive in their own minds that they are superior to others. The remnant is the cream of the crop, the survivors who have learned to thrive during the trial.

Many biblical examples illustrate how God separated a much smaller remnant from among the masses. He chose to anoint and bless the remnant because they were loyal, faithful, and true to the Word of God, to Christ, and to the builders of His kingdom.

In Israel's ancient history, during a national crisis, only one man, Elijah, resisted the corrupt governmental leadership of Ahab and Jezebel. One man stood up to confront the evil control of this group of anti-God covenant breakers. Righteous prophets were being executed or threatened with death if they spoke, so the warning voices were being silenced. This caused a national split between two opposing views, reminding me of America's 50-50 split in opinions. Like Israel, the US is stuck between two opinions, or conflicting worldviews (1 Kings 18:21).

God informed the discouraged prophet that there were seven thousand prophets who had not compromised, but they were not fulfilling their calling because they were too intimidated to stand up or speak out. Eventually, though, Ahab and Jezebel were defeated by the Jehu spirit and the remnant emerged from the cave.

Those who desire to be part of the end-time faithful remnant, those who will not bow to a manmade antichrist system, must find others of like faith. Unite in prayer, support one another, and promote the Kingdom of God. His kingdom will eventually swallow up the kingdoms of this world, and one day His kingdom will rule the nations of the world (Rev 11:15; 21:5).

It is no time to be spiritually asleep; it is time to be awake and sober (1 Peter 5:8).

CHAPTER 19

WHEN POLITICAL LEADERS HAVE NO DIVINE FAVOR

Over the decades that I have spent in ministry, my peers and at times denominational leaders have been at odds with my non-traditional approach to ministry. I never have fit into any structured, man-made, or traditional mold. I'm a fourth-generation minister who stepped away from the usual path when I began to study and teach the Hebraic roots of Christianity, and occasionally use ancient rabbinical methods to study prophecy and patterns. The traditional Full Gospel community was unfamiliar with these methods, so it left open a door for criticism, as we often criticize what we do not understand.

I have used several of these unusual methods when projecting what I believed would be *patterns* of cyclical history, including history repeated from the past for America's future leaders. During past presidential elections, often before the person won or was sworn in, through prayer, historical research, and the study of parallels discovered in Old Testament stories, I would predict the type of leadership and certain events that would occur during their administration. Another method considered controversial was to take the English name, translate it into Hebrew, or take the year they were elected on the Hebrew calendar, and exchange the Hebrew letters for their numerical values or the numerical values for the Hebrew letters, and discover words that related to events, cycles, or patterns of their election or administration.

For several consecutive years, in the fall months when the Jewish calendar changes, I have taken the numbers of the Jewish New Year (Rosh Hashanah) and used the symbols of the Hebrew letters assigned to the numbers to reveal the primary spiritual attack, blessing, or activity for the coming year. Many people, myself included, have been amazed at the accuracy of each prediction and how situations aligned so well with the patterns. In Revelation, John used a system like this when he instructed the reader to count (or calculate) the number of the beast (Antichrist), for it is 666 (Rev. 13:17-18).

I have noticed that these methods are most accurate during major prophetic cycles. I will share with you how I used one of these methods to show that Donald Trump would come out on top in the 2016 election.

THE NUMBER 45 AND TRUMP

Political polls, up to the night of the 2016 election, were against Donald Trump. Media pundits everywhere were predicting a Hillary Clinton win. However, using the system I have referred to, I saw where the outcome could be different.

The next United States president would be the forty-fifth. In the Hebrew alphabet, each letter has a number value attached to it. The Hebrew letter with the value of 40 is *mem*, and the letter with the value of 5 is *hei*. Putting the two letters together, it spells the Hebrew word *ma*, which in Hebrew means, "What?" The clue here is that whoever won the election as the 45th president would have people saying, "What? What? How did this happen?"

I taught this in three public meetings in 2016 before the election: during the summer at the Field House in Williamson, West Virginia; in La Marque, Texas at Walter Hallam's church; and the night of the election at Omega Center International in Cleveland, Tennessee, one hour before any election results started coming in. Eventually, Trump was declared the winner. Two days later, I was watching Fox News when one of the commentators was talking about people being in shock that Trump won. She commented, "People in America are saying to themselves, 'What happened? How did Trump win this election?'"

ADMINISTRATIONS OF DISFAVOR

In 2020, the crowds in every state were so large for Trump and so low or non-existent for Biden that most Americans believed Trump would win by a landslide, despite what the pollsters, pundits, and prognosticators were predicting.

On election night, in the five states that Trump needed to win, the numbers began to shift. In some states, election officials ran poll observers out of the building, even covering up windows so none of them could see inside. Machines were shut down in the middle of the night, during which time huge numbers of Biden votes were added to the count. By the next morning, Biden had mysteriously obtained a massive and historically high number of votes, with a mere five counties putting him over the top. Somehow, the man who showed increasing signs of dementia, who campaigned from his basement, and who many suggest should have been disqualified due to his connections with the Chinese Communist Party, managed to get the largest number of votes in history. The gleeful media couldn't wait to announce that Biden won and Trump lost.

I will not use this book to explain the brazen levels of state and county voter fraud that occurred, the countless irregularities that existed, or the illegal foreign interference in our election, as several individuals have spent thousands of hours and millions of dollars to examine this in detail. I am focusing instead on what this type of activity would be considered from a biblical perspective. It would be considered manipulation, covetousness, fraud, injustice, and an unjust balance.

According to a recent Rasmussen poll, there are two groups: the 39% of likely voters who believe it was unlikely that cheating affected the outcome of the election, and the 56% who believe it's likely or highly likely that cheating affected the outcome. The more we learn about election fraud, the more people believe the outcome was organized by criminal elements working in conjunction with leaders of certain other countries to remove President Trump because he was a hindrance to the implementation of the globalist agenda for a great reset and world domination.

If we accept the evidence that has been uncovered by people who have investigated the 2020 election, and if we accept the growing volume of proof that the election outcome was fraudulent, then from a biblical perspective, what is God's view of the situation? And if stolen, why would God allow it? What does that mean for America, in the seasons we are in and the seasons that will follow in years to come?

When national leaders do the *right things* based upon God's laws, when they make wise decisions militarily, economically, and socially, and when they help bring relief and freedom to the citizens, they receive favor with God. Favor is when the Almighty extends additional grace and the help that leaders need to overcome difficult challenges. We want leaders who keep us under the favorable blessings of God, and not under the national curses He warns of in Deuteronomy 28.

First, let's compare facts between the administrations of Donald Trump and Joe Biden. Here is a short list of President Trump's accomplishments during his presidency, until the time the virus struck the United States:

- The American economy was in a strong recovery.

- Jobs were returning to the United States from Mexico and overseas.

- Historically high levels of African American and Hispanic American employment were occurring, while poverty rates of both reached record lows.

- The country gained seven million new jobs and unemployment reached 3.5%, the lowest level in a half-century.

- The tax code was changed to provide relief to the middle class, which helped increase middle class family income by nearly $6,000 a year.

- Actions were taken to secure our country against the influx of terrorists, gangs, and drug cartel members who crossed our porous borders.

- One-sided trade deals that negatively impacted the US were being changed.

- High level terrorists in the Middle East were being killed by precision strikes and ISIS had been defeated.

- The United States Embassy was moved from Tel-Aviv to Jerusalem, the capital of Israel.

- Four Arab nations signed peace and economic agreements with Israel, with others in line to do the same.

- The Keystone pipeline was approved, and other actions were taken, all of which helped America become energy independent and reduced the price of oil and gasoline for consumers.

- Three Supreme Court justices were appointed.

- Measures were taken to stem the crisis of human trafficking.

- Changes were made to support the sanctity of life and prevent government funding of abortions.

- Measures were taken to protect religious liberty and freedom of speech.

- America was once again respected by both our enemies and allies as a leader among nations.

Covid-19 brought lockdowns and forced all but the largest businesses to close, especially in leftist-controlled states. I won't spend time here discussing the virus, its origins, or how it spread, but research seems to indicate that it was intentionally created and spread—both to destroy global economies and to wreck the successes of the Trump administration. The virus swept the United States and the world, and President Trump worked to help the country and stop the spread of the virus. We all might not agree with the outcomes of his work in that regard, but most would say he did the best he thought possible under the circumstances and with the advice he received.

Yet, despite everything he accomplished during his term in office, every member of the opposing party, and even some within his own party, cabinet, and other branches of government, did everything in their power to remove him from office, or to ensure that nothing he did would prosper. Greedy and power-hungry globalists, many of whom do not even live in the United States, had too much at stake to allow President Trump to destroy their plans for a premature world takeover.

THE BIDEN CONFUSION

It was evident very early during the campaign that Joe Biden had severe physical and mental challenges. At times he appeared so confused that, even in his prepared teleprompter speeches, his statements were bizarre and jumbled. More importantly, look at what America has dealt with since Joe Biden and Kamala Harris took office:

- The economy has been shaken and remains very unstable.

- Biden and Congress approved the spending of trillions of dollars in just the first few months that he held office.

- Inflation has skyrocketed, and gasoline prices shot up by 40 - 60%, almost overnight.

- He killed our energy independence.

- More Americans are receiving government assistance.

- Covid-related problems have gotten worse instead of better.

- Medical and other types of tyranny are being forced upon the entire population.

- Afghanistan was handed over to the Taliban, the same group once led by Osama Bin Laden. We left behind American citizens, Afghan citizens who helped our country, and military equipment worth billions of dollars.

- The nation is intentionally being divided along issues such as race, gender, masks, medical treatments, vaccines, vaccine mandates, vaccine passports, and any other problems that can be manufactured and hammered into the public's mind on a near-daily basis.

- The administration is allowing supply chain problems that are causing shortages that impact individuals, businesses, entire industries, food establishments, and jobs. As of this writing, cargo ships are sitting along the West and East Coasts and not being allowed into ports with their goods.

- Housing prices are skyrocketing, having increased 30 - 40% in some areas.

- Noted retailers are closing stores permanently.

- There is real danger that hyperinflation will destroy the value of the US dollar.

- The most liberal abortion laws on record are again being passed.

- An unprecedented crisis is occurring at our border, and both Biden and Harris refuse to take responsibility or stop it.

- People are fleeing leftist-controlled states as they search for a location that is run by sane leaders.

- Biden's cognitive disabilities have reached the point that our entire nation has become disrespected around the world, and a joke to leaders and citizens everywhere.

- Americans cannot figure out who is really in charge of the country.

When comparing these two lists, we clearly see a vast difference between the blessings and the curses that a nation can experience, based upon the leadership of the country.

Evildoers will use any means possible to manipulate votes and achieve their desired outcome; but when they do, there will be no divine favor upon them. God will not bless cheating and injustice. It is impossible for the Almighty to cancel His own laws and warnings to accommodate those who break His rules.

THE MEANING OF BIDEN'S NAME

Sometimes the parents of a newborn child will select a name for their boy or girl that has a special meaning. Throughout Scripture, the name of a child was believed to carry significance, and often the name concealed a message related to the child's birth or some important future assignment God planned for them.

One biblical example is Jacob, a son of Isaac and the father of twelve sons who formed the twelve tribes of Israel. He married two wives, and his favorite wife, Rachel, birthed two sons. Joseph was her first son, and years later Rachel died giving birth to her second son. As she was dying, a midwife asked her to name her newborn son. She called him Ben-oni, which in Hebrew means *son of my sorrow*. Jacob immediately rejected that, changing the newborn's name to Ben-jamin, meaning *son of my right hand* (Gen. 35:18). Throughout history, the tribe of Benjamin would remain faithful to the tribe of Judah, and both tribes' land grants bordered the temple in Jerusalem. Saul, Israel's first king, was from the tribe of Benjamin.

Biden's first name is not Joe, but Joseph. He was born in 1942, which was the height of World War II and the time of the horrific Nazi Holocaust. When translated into Hebrew, the name "Biden" can be divided into the Hebrew letters beit and yod, creating the Hebrew word that means "alas." The last two Hebrew letters in his name are daleth and nun, which is the Hebrew word for "Dan." One of Jacob's twelve sons was called Dan, and his name means *judge* or *judgment*. Therefore, using the rabbinic system of the meaning of names, the name Biden in Hebrew hints at the phrase *"alas, judgement."*

Under the Biden administration, we see natural disasters, our enemies rising above us, plagues increasing, economic problems growing, freedom disappearing, and leaders creating division and chaos. Can we as Christians acknowledge that these negative events can all be biblical signs of a national crisis caused by the leaders of our nation rejecting God and His rule of law?

Here is another view of this scenario. History indicates that God's will is not always done, including when it involves the selection of leaders. Look at a mistake Moses made. Instead of going directly into the Promised Land, he allowed twelve spies to take forty days to bring back a report (Numbers 13). Two of them, Joshua and Caleb, believed the people could take the land because God promised it. But ten spies saw the giants and walled cities. They brought back an evil report, saying it was too hard to war against the people. Instead of obeying God, the people of Israel voted with their unbelief and ended up wandering in a desert, going in circles, for one generation of forty years.

Christ chose twelve disciples. When Judas committed suicide, the remaining eleven held a business meeting and cast lots for a replacement. They chose a man who was never heard from again, anywhere in the New Testament. Had they not voted, years later the Apostle Paul would have been God's choice to replace Judas. He was an eyewitness of Christ, who appeared to him on the road to Damascus. Did the disciples miss the perfect will of God?

It is possible that America received the *permissible* will of God in 2020, and not God's choice, or *perfect* will. Under the early Old Testament theocracy, the priesthood was passed down from father to son, with heredity determining the king next in line for rulership.

However, the true prophets and priests originally anointed the leaders, without a vote from the people.

That would never work in America. The self-proclaimed prophets from one side of the aisle and the team of seers from the other side of the aisle would battle it out, each claiming to have the man that God has appointed. Without prayer and seeking the will of God, men like Hitler can be installed into power, thus leading a nation into an abyss of war, tyranny, death, and despair.

What happens when the wrong person is in power, whether by voting or manipulation? What happens when carnal men make the choices for a nation, and leave prayer and God out of the mix?

SAUL'S ADMINISTRATION FAILED

We can look for similar parallels in biblical narratives to answer those questions. One example is Saul, Israel's first king. God's will, or intent for Israel, was a *theocracy*, defined as a form of government in which God is recognized as the supreme civil ruler of the state, and His laws are taken as the statute-book of the kingdom. God wanted a spiritual kingdom, one in which the individual people (a holy nation) were a kingdom of priests (Exod. 19:6).

This form of government was directed by inspiration of the Holy Spirit, working through the minds and voices of priests and prophets. This is how the scriptures were written, as Paul noted when he wrote, "All scripture is given by inspiration of God..." (2 Tim. 3:16), and "Holy men of God spoke as they were moved by the Holy Spirit" (2 Pet. 1:21).

Occasionally, Israel would observe someone who came under this divine inspiration and mark them as anointed, which led the elders to appoint the anointed person as a judge. This fact is recorded throughout the biblical book of Judges.

Israel was surrounded by tribes and nations whose governments were monarchies, each led by a single king and his appointed leaders (Gen. 14:1-9). The nations would move from cycles of peace to seasons of wars and uprisings, then back to seasons of peace. The type of cycle was often determined by the actions or spiritual leadership of the judge.

The people of Israel became weary of self-government under a theocracy, as well as the corruption among some leaders, and began to demand a king like the other nations (1 Sam. 8:5). Samuel the prophet sought the Lord, who answered him and revealed that the people of Israel had now rejected God as their source and leader, and they turned to man instead. God told Samuel to protest what the people were demanding and warn them that their new king will put their sons and daughters into bondage (including financial bondage). He will focus upon himself, corrupt the military, and eventually seize their possessions and land for government use (1 Sam. 8:1-22). God's warning can be summed up in this sentence: *I will give you what you want, but eventually you will not like what you got!* Their first king was Saul, from the tribe of Benjamin, and Benjamin was the brother of Joseph.

At first, the people were relieved and excited to get behind their new leader. However, Saul began to make careless decisions. History indicates that Saul was a weak leader, especially from a military standpoint. He eventually lost his anointing, but he told the prophet Samuel, "Honor me before the elders [leaders] of my people" (1 Sam. 15:30). Saul had no real concern for the people and their needs; he only wanted to be honored for his position.

Saul was afraid of war, and he permitted the Philistine giant Goliath to run his mouth, mock the Israelites, and intimidate their army. Saul had no stomach to fight real enemies, but he took on his political opponent, David, and fought him for thirteen years. In the beginning, Saul had no interest in leading the nation, but the people pressured him. God was left out and the entire nation suffered.

After years of Saul's rule, his inability to make decisions, and his continual attacks on David, Scripture reveals what happened to Israel. The people rejected Saul and wanted David as king:

> *"And every one that was in distress, and every one that was in debt, and every one that was discontented, gathered themselves unto him; and he became a captain over them: and there were with him about four hundred men."*
>
> – 1 SAMUEL 22:2 (KJV)

We all understand debt, created by spending on things we cannot afford. The Hebrew word for *discontented* means bitterness in the soul (caused by anger). The Hebrew word for *distress* alludes to a very narrow place of hardship from which one is unable to escape or turn around. Today we would say we are stuck in one spot and nothing good is happening. We are in a situation that creates frustration and stress.

Saul was the choice of the people. Saul was *not* the perfect will of God; but he was the *permissible* will. God's permissible will is a concept that means He could intervene, but He will not, as people made the decision or choice in the matter. They wanted their desire, not God's desire. For example, in the Torah, God instructed Israel to "choose this day." God has revealed His will through His written Word, but He will not force it upon us, as we are given free will and the ability to choose.

As for the election of Joe Biden, several theories have circulated in the Body of Christ. One says the election was stolen, another says that God got rid of Trump, and another says that vote manipulation may have occurred, but God's purposes will still be accomplished.

Based on the laws and principles of Scripture, beginning with the Torah, if tyrannical agents worked from the inside to corrupt the election and substitute their own agenda for God's will, here is what this means: God does not go against His written laws, statutes, and judgments, even though cultural ideas, traditions, and methods change throughout the generations. He tells us in Scripture that certain actions are a sin.

It is possible that the present situation demands that God's hand of favor and blessing be lifted off the nation, as the Almighty cannot go against His own rules of punishment for the iniquities and abominations that are occurring. The Father in Heaven, including under the new covenant of redemption, cannot and will not bless theft and deceit, either spiritually or politically.

Said another way, God blesses His plans, but He does not bless any of man's plans that are contrary to His purpose or will. God will allow arrogant, unbelieving men to fail and fall flat on their faces, thereby causing them and the nation to struggle and experience humiliation. This gives an opportunity for national repentance and a return to the blessing of God. As I observe the situation, it seems that America has reached a peak of iniquity, and when God wants to judge a nation, He allows them to have unwise and unscrupulous leaders.

THE STORM IS OUT THERE

Being out of God's predestined purpose can and will create unplanned storms. This lesson was learned when a ship full of prisoners that included the Apostle Paul scheduled a winter departure to Rome. During winter, the Mediterranean Sea experiences violent storms. Paul warned the ship's owner and others that the timing for the journey was wrong. He said, "Men, I perceive that this voyage will end with disaster and much loss, not only of the cargo and ship, but also our lives." The centurion was more persuaded by the master and owner of the ship, so they ignored Paul's warnings and sailed into contrary winds (Acts 27:11-15).

The result was a storm that was so bad the sun and stars were not observed for fourteen days, which sent the ship into unknown directions. The vessel was storm-tossed. They had to throw cargo overboard. Violent waves broke the ship apart, plunging 276 men into icy waters, where they eventually floated to an island on broken boards from a wrecked ship (Acts 27).

Perhaps the ship's owner would have listened to Paul had Paul been a ship owner and not a preacher. Ministers are often ignored as irrelevant or misguided voices that represent a relic religion. We warn, but few listen. Daniel said that none of the wicked will understand, but the wise will understand (Dan. 12:10).

The infamous biblical king Ahab was warned that he would die in an upcoming battle. Thinking he could prevent the fulfillment of this prediction, Ahab exchanged his kingly robes with those of another king, Jehoshaphat, to disguise himself from the opposing army. Despite his attempt at deception, an arrow struck Ahab between the joints of his armor while he was in his chariot. He died that day, fulfilling the prophetic warning given twenty-four hours earlier (2 Chron. 18).

If Biden does not serve out his entire term, the next person in line for the presidency is Harris, who would be America's first female president. When Ahab was removed from office (through death) his wife took control of the country. Harris is not Biden's wife, of course, but it's an interesting observation.

A WORD ABOUT BIDEN

In the early morning of October 2, 2021, as this book was in the editing stage, I heard a still, small voice speak a word to me about Biden and his administration. The word I received from the Lord that morning was: "Their table shall become a snare."

That comes from Psalm 69:22-23: "Let their table become a snare before them, and that which should have been for their welfare, let it become a trap. Let their eyes be darkened, that they see not; And make their loins continually to shake."

In biblical days, the table was where the kings would meet and make decisions. A snare was a device used to trap unsuspecting animals. In context, David had been going through serious personal trials and a flood of troubles. A lot of people despised him for some decisions he made. People in political leadership positions were working behind the scenes to hinder David's administration and keep him from accomplishing the things he wanted to do.

In these verses, David was crying out to the Lord, and the response he received was that he should not worry about those who were doing this undercover work. Their own table—their own secret meetings and strategizing—were going to become their own snare.

This is how I interpret the word about Biden. Those who are behind the scenes secretly strategizing against the people might feel secure in their plots, but as they are making their plans, something is going to cause those strategies to become their own snare. They think they are setting a trap for others, but instead they are setting a trap for themselves. The Lord seems to be saying that everything Biden and those around him are doing and planning will fail and backfire. They will be caught in their own trap.

As I write this, we are seeing the chaotic results of bizarre decisions made by this administration. We are being told that we don't have freedom to make our own decisions; we must obey their system. People are losing their jobs because of tyrannical threats coming from the administration, and because large corporations are obeying these threats in violation of our own Constitution.

It is unknown exactly how things will unfold in the future. However, with the increase in prophetic signs being fulfilled and a nation in disfavor, all believers must remember that we belong to the Kingdom of God. We are a nation within a nation, a kingdom within a kingdom, and our government is not of this present world. We must endure and fight the good fight of faith. In the end, we win.

CHAPTER 20

DONALD TRUMP AND SECOND TERM HISTORICAL PARALLELS

P atterns and parallels are interesting and sometimes meaningful because, in Ecclesiastes 1:9-10, Solomon reminded future generations that the thing which has been, is that which shall be, and that which was done (in the past) shall be done again (in the future). In other words, history repeats itself.

In the past, I have researched historical patterns and parallels between presidents. Some of the most interesting parallels were between Abraham Lincoln and John F. Kennedy:

- Both were elected to Congress, 100 years apart: Lincoln in 1846 and Kennedy in 1946.

- Both were elected president 100 years apart: 1860 and 1960.

- Both vice presidents were named Johnson, and both were born 100 years apart: Andrew Johnson in 1808 and Lyndon Johnson in 1908. Both men were Democrat senators from the South before they became vice presidents.

- Both experienced the death of a son while serving in the White House.

- Both foresaw their deaths before they occurred; both were shot on a Friday; both were shot in the head; and both were shot in the presence of their wives.

- Personal secretaries of both Lincoln and Kennedy warned them to change their plans on the days they were assassinated.

- Lincoln was shot in a theater and the killer hid in a barn; Kennedy was shot from a warehouse and the killer hid in a theater.

- Both assassins were killed before they stood trial.

There are also some patterns between Lincoln and Obama, but it is unclear if some of these events were done intentionally for the optics:

- Both were born outside of Illinois but later moved to the state. Both were lawyers who practiced in the state.

- Lincoln served 8 years in the House and Obama 8 years in the Illinois State Senate.

- Obama was born 100 years after Lincoln became President (1861 and 1961)

- Obama was inaugurated 200 years after Lincoln's birth (1809 and 2009)

- Obama delivered a speech at the opening of the Abraham Lincoln Presidential Museum.

- Obama attended the grand re-opening of the Ford Theatre on February 11, 2009.

- Obama took a 137-mile train ride from Philadelphia to Washington, mirroring Lincoln's inaugural ride.

- Obama took office on the same Bible as Lincoln, called the Lincoln Bible.

- Obama dined on replica plates that Lincoln used at his inaugural dinner.

We also find a few parallels between Kennedy and Obama:

- Both were senators (Kennedy was a U.S. Senator and Obama an Illinois State Senator).

- Both were elected in their 40s, which was considered a young age.

- Both wrote books before they became President.

- Both attended Harvard and were lawyers.

- Both campaigned on a theme of hope and change.

These comparisons show examples of commonalities that involve repetitive historical patterns. But what about Donald Trump? Are there historical patterns between him and any previous president?

From the time that George Washington served as America's first president until today, there have been forty-six presidencies, with forty-five different people serving as President of the United States. There has been only one president who lost his reelection bid to his opponent, yet returned four years later to be reelected by the American people. That man was President Grover Cleveland.

Cleveland's first years of service were 1885 to 1889. He campaigned for reelection and lost to Benjamin Harrison. Four years later, he ran again and was elected to serve a second term from 1893 to 1897. What makes this historic pattern interesting is the possibility of Donald Trump running for a second term after a four-year gap.

Are there any interesting parallels between Grover Cleveland and Donald Trump? Here are some that emerge:

- Both had a Presbyterian background. Cleveland's father was a Presbyterian minister, and Trump was Presbyterian. Trump also has a family connection on his mother's side to the great Hebrides revival in Scotland.

- Both have a New York connection. Both were raised there, and New York was the primary home of Trump until he changed his status to Florida.

- Both were recognized for their ability to focus intently on whatever task faced them and see it through to a resolution.

- Cleveland's wife was 27 years younger, and Melania was 24 years younger than Trump.

- Opponents of both Cleveland and Trump refused to acknowledge the attributes of the First Ladies because they despised the President so much. One of Cleveland's foes said, "I detest him so much that I don't even think his wife is beautiful." Melania Trump was mocked by her husband's detractors, and she graced the covers of no magazines during her husband's presidential term, despite her elegance and past career as a model.

- Both ran as political reformers and were considered such by the citizens.

- Both fought political corruption and fiercely guarded the integrity of the office in which they served.

- Both made many powerful enemies for their actions against crime and dishonesty, which would later cost both men their reelection.

- Both pursued policies that barred special favors to certain groups.

- Both had controversies concerning women and accusations leveled against them.

- Both had their opposing parties attempt to use accusations to politically defeat them.

- Both angered certain union organizations.

- Both were considered pro-business.

- Both battled pork barrel politics.

- Both were considered self-reliant.

- Both refused to cower to the progressives of their day.

- Both, at times, defied the expectations of their own party for the benefit of Americans.

- Both avoided personally fighting in wars (Cleveland, the Civil War; Trump, the Vietnam War), and both were opposed to useless and endless wars.

- Both preferred that people have personal economic opportunities instead of paternal care from the government because it strengthens both character and the nation.

- Both had people from within their own political party turn against them in public.

- Both used tariffs to strengthen the economy.

- In their first terms, both had vice presidents from Indiana (although Thomas Hendricks died before his term ended).

- Both vice presidents were lawyers who had served as governors of Indiana and represented their state in the House of Representatives.

- Both had controversies that surrounded their Supreme Court nominees.

- In both elections, there was talk and accusations of voter fraud.

- Both were known as the hardest working presidents of their generation, and both routinely worked past midnight, often until two or three o'clock in the morning.

- Cleveland paid his own expenses, and Trump did not take a salary during his presidency.

Cleveland was reelected for a second, non-consecutive term, which he won by a decisive margin—277 electoral votes to Harrison's 145. As that term began, he found himself having to deal with a severe national economic depression caused by the Panic of 1893. He had to deal with the Treasury crisis while the country was facing business failures, farm mortgage foreclosures, and unemployment.

As I write this, all economic indicators during the Biden administration point to the country facing another severe economic depression. If Trump indeed serves a second term, he could find himself dealing with the same kind of national economic hardships that Cleveland dealt with in his second term.

Biographer Allan Nevins wrote that Grover Cleveland possessed honesty, courage, firmness, independence, and common sense to a degree that other men do not. By the end of his second term, he was an unpopular president. But historians now look back on Cleveland and consider him a successful leader who is praised for his honesty, integrity, adherence to his morals, effective leadership, and defiance of party boundaries. He is ranked in the upper-mid tier of American presidents.

Will we see a repeat of these parallels under a second presidential term of Donald Trump? Time will tell.

BIDEN – HARRIS – HARRISON

The politician who defeated Cleveland was named Benjamin Harrison. As noted earlier, in biblical history, Benjamin was the youngest brother of Joseph. It was Joseph Biden who was placed in office in 2021. Biden's Vice President, Kamala, has the last name Harris. That might be a superficial pattern at this point, but it seems interesting to me.

Are there any parallels between Joseph Biden and Benjamin Harrison? There are a few:

- Harrison conducted a front-porch campaign, where people came to Indianapolis and heard him give speeches. Biden conducted a basement campaign, where he stood before a camera in his basement and gave speeches.

- When Harrison attributed his win to Providence, political boss Matt Quay responded that Harrison would never know "how close a number of men were compelled to approach... the penitentiary to make him President." It sounds as though there might have been corruption and election fraud in the Harrison win, just as we see being exposed in the Biden win.

- Harrison signed large appropriations bills, and for the first time except in war, Congress appropriated a billion dollars. The Federal budget exploded. The same thing is happening in the Biden administration, only this time the numbers have increased to multiple trillions.

- Before the end of Harrison's administration, the Treasury surplus had evaporated, and prosperity was disappearing as well. In just the first year of the Biden administration, the economy is continuing to tank as we experience high inflation and industry-wide supply chain disruptions that are destroying the prosperity of average Americans and small business owners.

- Historians rank Harrison as below-average, primarily because of the corruption in his administration. Comparatively, there seems to be much corruption in the Biden administration, and most people wouldn't question where he will stand on the historical ranking scale.

WILL DONALD TRUMP RETURN?

Due to Donald Trump aligning with patterns of Grover Cleveland, the only president who lost his second term and won again four years later, it would be no surprise if Trump ran and won in the 2024 election. If that happens, many will say that America's presidential history has repeated itself.

CHAPTER 21

FINAL ATTACKS ON CHRISTIANS AND CHURCHES

Toward the conclusion of writing these visions, I was strongly impressed to add the details of this vision as well. This is the only vision I will share in this book that was not experienced by either my father or myself. This one was told to me by a young man who was run over by a car as a child and survived. I heard it when I was preaching in Deland, Florida years ago. It is my opinion that the church has now entered the season indicated in the vision. The young man told me that the vision will come to pass toward the conclusion of the church age.

At the beginning of this vision, this young man observed a massive field of grain with a blue hue. It was a beautiful day and there was a huge army of people, marching in step and in order. Everyone was smiling and appeared happy.

Suddenly, out of nowhere, the sky became full of vultures coming from every direction, headed toward this army. I was reminded of Mark 4:4, where the birds come into the field and devour the seed of the Word before it can take root in the heart of the listener. In the parable, the birds stealing the seed represent Satan and his kingdom seizing the Word from the heart (Mark 4:15). In the vision, the vultures began to drop things, scattering them throughout the field. At times, whatever they dropped was visible to a person once they came upon it; at other times, the objects were hidden.

These vultures were dropping three different objects onto the field: tares, stones, and missiles.

The tares were placed in the field to stop the harvest, or to make it more difficult to harvest the pure grain. Christ gave a parable of the wheat and tares, in which He identified the wheat as children of His Kingdom and the tares as children of Satan. Both will grow together in the same field, and at the final harvest the angels will separate the wheat (good) from the tares (bad). A farmer does not want to mingle the harvest of pure grain, as the tares are bitter and can be poisonous, causing sickness or even death.

Tares would also allude to all forms of false teaching that would emerge in the body of Christ toward the time of the end. We currently see an entire generation with little or no biblical knowledge. They are easily swayed by fads and trends, including tolerance toward any type of sin, iniquity, or abomination that is forbidden in the Bible. Paul warned that in the latter times, "Some shall depart from the faith, giving heed to seducing spirits, and doctrines of devils" (1 Tim. 4:1).

The stones were hidden and scattered throughout the field for the purpose of making a soldier in God's army stumble. These stones were different sizes, and some had the name of a person carved on them. When someone tripped over one of these stones, the person fell to the ground wounded and was unable to get up. This is when the vultures specifically targeted them.

The stones, or stumbling blocks, include anything that would cause a brother or sister to stumble. Consider this example: in the New Testament there were two divisive teachings. The first was circumcision, which almost split the church between the Jews, who demanded circumcision, and the Gentiles, who did not feel obligated to perform circumcision. The second was eating meat. Gentile cities sold meat in the markets that had been sacrificed on pagan altars. Paul taught to eat what was set before you, asking no questions "for conscience' sake" (1 Cor. 10:27). He also taught that, if you eat or drink anything that would cause a brother or sister to stumble, avoid it (Rom. 14:13). Some Christians claim they have a new liberty to do what others cannot. However, Paul taught that we should not use our liberty to cause a weak brother or sister to stumble (1 Cor. 8:9). He wrote, "When you sin against the brethren, and wound their weak conscience, you sin against Christ" (1 Cor. 8:12).

While the enemy may set stumbling blocks before us, we should never ourselves become the stumbling block. We don't always do something just because we can, or because we don't have a particular conviction about it. We should consider the other people we may influence.

In the claws of many of the vultures was some type of missile. These missiles were the darts that the Apostle Paul warned about in Ephesians 6. They are the "fiery darts of the enemy" that must be quenched by the shield of faith (Eph. 6:16).

The missiles are a different type of assault, as they can originate in the mind. Any thought that becomes a stronghold that you must pull down is an arrow, or a dart (in Greek, a missile) of the adversary (Eph. 6:16). Then the missile is ignited, becoming a fiery dart, and the struggle increases. A dart on fire is a burning thought, or a mental obsession that you cannot get rid of easily.

THE SCENE CHANGED

In the vision, the army came under so many attacks from different directions that, instead of uniting, they began to divide in the field. The vultures seemed to become stronger. The biggest danger was for anyone who separated themselves from a group and tried to go it alone.

Several different scenes emerged.

The first scene was an elderly grandmother who held up a shield in front of her to prevent any missiles from directly hitting her. She had several grandchildren who were not taking things seriously and were running around in front of the shield as though they were playing a game. Suddenly the children were hit by darts and fell to the ground. They each needed their own shield (of faith) to stand against the enemy. However, they were leaning on the grandmother's faith to protect and help them.

One man who had no shield or protection was running through the field, thinking he could outrun the warfare that was unfolding around him. He suddenly was knocked to the ground as he tripped on something hidden in his path. He was unaware that the sudden attack would take him off his feet. This type of attack is evident with people who are suddenly missing in action in the Body of Christ after allowing the adversary to defeat them.

In a third scene from the field, another individual seemed to be doing well walking through the field, when suddenly he was not watching and tripped over a stone that had his name on it. He stumbled and fell on his face, lying alone for a few moments. Without warning, several vultures swooped down and began picking at his flesh as though to devour him. This was a clear symbol that this man's flesh (carnality) would eventually capture him, and he would not be able to escape. He had no armor on and no shield up.

The young man told me that, in the vision, he would see breaks between battles. There would be groups of people that would be together, smiling, laughing, singing, and worshipping. There were not always struggles in the field. There were seasons of joy and breakthrough, as victories were being won by those willing to stand and fight. This reminded me of when Christ taught that, when we ask, He will answer, that our joy might be full (John 16:24).

After the three scenes, suddenly a man on a white horse appeared in the distance, toward the edge of the field. He was a false Christ and not the true Messiah. Some Christians broke rank and began following the man on the horse. Despite what appeared to be confusion and defeat in so many areas, there remained a strong and determined remnant.

In the final scene, the remnant began to dig a trench to battle the vultures and protect themselves from assault. The last fight would be the biggest yet. About the time the battle was set in array and both sides would clash, the remnant looked up and saw the city of God appear in heaven. They knew the end had come and the Lord was prepared to take them to the heavenly city.

WHAT WE MUST DO

It is evident that this vision was an important word from the Lord to the church. The question is, what can we do to be strong in these days and complete our race and assignment? I suggest these four keys.

1. Minister to the Wounded

Many individuals have experienced what I call sacred scars, or wounds they have received from Christians. The Body of Christ should be the safest place on earth for an emotionally wounded or hurting individual. However, the church is filled with wounded men and women who still carry unhealed scars and who, at times, either intentionally or unwittingly wound others with their actions or words.

Jesus spoke of leaving the flock of ninety-nine sheep to find the one sheep that has strayed (Matt. 18:12-13). In another parable, a Samaritan, a man who in Christ's day was considered a minority and despised among religious Jews, came across a stranger who had been wounded by thieves. The Samaritan carried the man to an inn and poured on the wine (to kill bacteria) and the oil (to help heal the wound), helping the victim recover.

The wounded need a healer and healing. We must focus on finding the lost sheep, and not just feeding the ninety-nine sheep.

2. Stay United and Not Divided

A special anointing is released when people are in unity. In Acts 2:1-4, when the Holy Spirit was poured out on the Day of Pentecost, they were in one accord. We also read how believers in the early church had all things in common (Acts 2:44). Paul spoke of the unity of the Spirit (Eph. 4:3), along with the unity of the faith (Eph. 4:13). If one can chase a thousand and two in agreement can chase ten thousand (Deut. 32:30), then when more believers join in unity, the power of agreement increases our level of spiritual authority against all dark forces.

Christ revealed that, "Every kingdom divided against itself is brought to desolation, and a house divided against itself cannot stand" (Matt. 12:25). Anything with two visions creates division, or a divided vision. Unity comes through faith and the Spirit.

3. Love One Another

Christ taught that we are His disciples if we love one another (John 13:34-35). Adversity and spiritual adversaries can never divide or defeat an assembly of people who truly care for and love one another. It is true that when you have trouble, you discover who your real friends are. Love covers a lot of faults. Some people will complain when someone else's children do the same things their own children are doing, yet they extend mercy to their own bloodline because love covers. Love never excuses failure but seeks restoration.

4. Keep Your Armor On

Paul gave an analogy of the Roman soldier's armor and compared each piece to spiritual armor for Christians. He noted the importance of being fully covered from head to foot so that we are able to withstand in the evil day (Eph. 6:13). The word *withstand* in Greek refers to *standing against* or *resisting* something, in this case standing when evil presents itself. The Greek word for *evil* is *poneros,* which is a time of malicious harm, anguish, and in a sense, moral danger.

In Ephesians 6:12-18, God's body armor is spiritual and invisible, but is applied by confessing the Word of God over your mind, heart, walk, and faith.

TAKE HEED

As believers we need to heed the warnings in this vision and always keep our spiritual armor on. Attacks will increase the closer we draw to the end of this age. If we remain united, lock our shields of faith with the shields of other believers, and love and care for one another, we can overcome the tares, stumbling stones, and missiles sent from the enemy. If we do this, we will find it much easier to endure and overcome.

CHAPTER 22

REVIVAL THROUGH THE LENS OF A CAMERA

This revelation I am sharing is the only one in this book that did not come to me in the form of a dream or night vision. I would consider it an inspired word from the Lord. This revelation has a great bearing upon where we are prophetically in relation to the gospel of the kingdom reaching all nations. It also explains an important ministry strategy that is available to help us fulfill Christ's prediction in Matthew 24:14, which says that the gospel will be preached as a witness unto all nations, and then the end will come.

Since 2011, our ministry has hosted livestreamed prayer over the internet from Cleveland, Tennessee each Thursday at 6:00 pm (EST). Our first prayer service began with a small group of ten youth in the upstairs of a remodeled barn on the Omega Center International (OCI) property located behind our ministry headquarters. Three small cameras were set up to capture prayer for internet viewers for one hour each Thursday.

Eventually it grew until between fifty to one hundred people of all ages gathered to intercede for the needs of people and the nation. From any location in the world, someone with a computer and internet access could e-mail us a prayer request, and we would print it and hand it to our prayer team, who would personally pray for the person's request.

People from around America and the world logged on, uniting their faith and prayers with ours.

Due to weather extremes, along with the difficulty of elderly folks climbing the stairs to the upper floor of the barn, we moved prayer from the barn to the small sanctuary at the Omega Center facility. From this room, our technical team used a single camera on a tripod to film and livestream prayer around the globe.

In January of 2019, before prayer began, I was standing in front of a small camera, adjusting the lens and positioning it to focus on the podium where a prayer leader would be directing the service. Instantly, I sensed a strong presence of the Lord overshadow me. For a moment, it was as though time stopped and I was standing there in body, but my inner spirit was alert and very sensitive to the Lord's voice. I clearly heard these words: *Revival will come through the lens of a camera!* I heard this inwardly, but also as though someone was speaking into my right ear. It was not coming from my mind, but from a heavenly dimension beyond time and space. I think this might have been John's experience on the island of Patmos when he wrote, "I was in the Spirit on the Lord's Day, and heard behind me a great voice...." (Rev. 1:10).

The statement about the lens of the camera immediately began to burn in my mind and spirit. I walked around the room, praying and meditating upon what I heard. That same night, I announced to the hundred or so people gathered in the room and hundreds watching online that revival was going to come through the lens of a camera. The people gladly received the message. However, none of us were certain exactly what this meant. At the time, I was in the process of building a new and contemporary prayer set with digital screens at our ISOW facility at the T.L. Lowery Global Center.

My interpretation at that time was that revival would come through the Thursday night prayer services being livestreamed. Our viewing audience had grown from a handful to hundreds and gradually thousands. But it would be one year later that the impact of this word became reality.

LOCKDOWNS AND LIMITED ATTENDANCE

As Covid-19 spread in 2020, we watched as federal, state, and local governments issued new rules regulating the number of attendees allowed in public gathering places and church sanctuaries. Federal government representatives claimed we needed to stay inside for two weeks to slow the spread of the virus and return to normal life, so most of the country was required to go on lockdown. In some places, large gatherings were restricted to only ten people in attendance at one time. In other places, people were not allowed to gather at all.

To our dismay, this ruling required that we cancel two large Warrior-Fest youth events in March and April that had 16,000 attendees registered. As we announced the cancellation, I remembered the prophetic word about the lens of a camera. This word inspired me to inform the bands and worship teams to prepare to do both Warrior-Fest conferences livestreamed from an empty building.

Before this time, we had never livestreamed any of our major conferences. Our ministry team was stunned when over 50,000 people from around the world logged online and watched both events. That is ten times the number of people who were registered to attend just one conference in our OCI facility. We were delighted to receive live reports of people receiving Christ, being filled with the Holy Spirit, and being healed. These two internet conferences made us realize the extent to which the anointing—the tangible energy of the Holy Spirit— has no limitations and can flow from people and buildings, through computers and smartphones, and touch the people watching.

A NEW END-TIME METHOD BIRTHED

At the end of 2020, my ministry office manager, Charlie Ellis, received a phone call from a noted minister in a large, Islamic nation. The minister believed the Lord had inspired him about the lens of the camera message, and he wanted to try something. He would organize a village meeting, set up a large screen on a platform, and use a certain system to connect with us. I would preach live from Cleveland, Tennessee, and he would interpret my message as the people sat in a large field and watched me speak on a screen from our location in Tennessee. It was almost like preaching in person on the platform in his nation.

The results were astonishing! Here is the text message we received the day following a lens of the camera event that was viewed by thousands of people gathered from villages:

> *"Over 15,000 people were in attendance as Pastor Stone was speaking. We are praising God that 8,395 souls received Christ for the first time. Over 200 in attendance testified to receiving some type of a physical healing, and another 586 people received the Holy Spirit baptism..."*

In eight months and through five events, over 35,000 previously unreached people in another nation have received Christ! Each new believer receives a Bible that our ministry purchases. This new type of evangelism was repeated throughout the year in other villages. Through Warrior-Fest events, world prayer each Thursday, and these overseas evangelistic events, *revival was coming through the lens of a camera!*

I started to consider how this method could be repeated in most nations of the world. The traditional method has been for an evangelist to drive to an airport, take a long journey in a plane, minister in person as many times as possible, then return home, exhausted. Yet through this new method, the travel expenses are nonexistent, and a minister can preach and see the same results, just as though physically present in that nation.

THE NEXT LEVEL

I believe this prophetic word is not just for foreign ministry events. It is possible that new viruses, future plagues, problems that create government mandated martial law, and so on could cause people again to be forced to remain in their homes or apartments, with their only connection to the outside world being their computers and phones.

From their home and an internet connection, a family can watch a live or recorded event from anywhere in the world. If people are forced into weeks or months of isolation, the only way the message of the gospel can reach them would be through the lens of a camera.

There is one great sign mentioned in the four Gospels that tells us what must happen before the end will come. The verse is Matthew 24:14: "This gospel of the kingdom shall be preached in all the world for a witness unto all nations; and then shall the end come." We are not told how the nations will be reached or what methods will be used; we only know that the message will be heard in all the world and all nations. Today, it is being heard—loud and clear.

CHAPTER 23

TEN RULES AND PRINCIPLES FOR SURVIVING AND THRIVING

A *rule* is a specific guideline or authoritative regulation that determines conduct and procedure. Rules govern a particular activity or sphere. A *principle* is a fundamental truth, law, or doctrine that serves as the foundation for a belief or behavior. The laws of God in the Bible are His rules. The biblical wisdom and instructions for daily living, such as we find written in Proverbs, are principles. They are proven guidelines to point you in the right direction and help you make the best choices.

In this chapter are ten proven and tested rules and principles to help you survive and thrive in the times we are in—times considered by most prophetic teachers to be *the last days* (2 Tim. 3:1; 2 Pet. 3:3) and *the time of the end* (Dan. 8:17; 12:9).

1. Do Not Compromise Your Convictions

A *conviction* is a firmly held belief of which you are so convinced, that it is settled in your mind and heart. Religious convictions based upon Scripture form your spiritual and moral values. Christians believe that some actions are right and others are wrong because they base their values and convictions upon the Word of God. The Bible reveals God's rules for life and laws for living. When a person is truly born again (John 3:3), the Almighty creates in them a new heart and a renewed mind. Old things will pass away, and all things will become new (2 Cor. 5:17)

If you touch hot metal, you will get burned and feel pain. When Samson flirted with Delilah, he started out teasing her to bind him with ropes and vines. Over time, he went from vines, to pins in his hair, to exposing his Nazarite vow and the secret of his seven locks of hair, which ended up on Delilah's floor before sunrise. Samson, who once was God's superhero, was now a weakling with his eyes gouged out, forced into slavery in a Philistine grain house.

David kept his *heart* on God but his *eyes* on a married woman. Jesus said, "The light of the body is the eye" (Matt. 6:22). Christ also taught that when a man looks on a woman with lustful intentions, he has already committed adultery in his heart (Matt. 5:28).

Compromise is a short cut to disaster. If you tend to follow the crowd and let down your guard, just remember that the wide path leads to eternal destruction (Matt 7:13).

2. Keep the Wrong Doors Closed

In Revelation, Christ tells the church at Philadelphia that He set before them an open door that no man can shut (Rev. 3:8). A door figuratively refers to an *opportunity* before you, that by faith you must walk through. However, it is possible for us to keep the wrong doors open and give the wrong people (or spirits) access.

I once had a challenge completely forgiving some people from my heart. One morning, I received a call from Pastor Tony Scott, who had been praying for me that morning. He gave me this verse:

"When angry, do not sin; do not ever let your wrath (your exasperation, your fury or indignation) last until the sun goes down. Leave no [such] room or foothold for the devil [give no opportunity to him]."

— EPHESIANS 4:26-27 (AMP)

I had been angry, and the reason I was unable to gain total freedom is because I was keeping a door open. Every day, the sun was going down on my wrath, which allowed the devil a foothold to keep gaining access. My mental thoughts and occasional words allowed a spirit from the adversary to continue to harass me. My prayer of, "Lord, I forgive" was from my *head* and not my *heart* and spirit. Only when I stopped mentally rehearsing what if—what if I had done this, what if I had said that, what if I had exposed this—did the door finally close.

As this passage in Ephesians says, if you don't deal with your anger, and if you plan on enforcing your own retaliation or vengeance, God's favor and blessing will stop coming your way. Let God shut the door that no man can open.

In these last days, walk only through the doors that God opens. Keep the wrong people, wrong thinking, and wrong attitudes shut out of your mind and heart.

3. Only the Strong Will Stand

When Paul revealed the believer's armor in Ephesians 6, he wrote, "withstand in the evil day" (Eph. 6:13). The Greek word withstand is *anthistemi*, meaning to *oppose, resist, or stand against*. Just as we must stand for some things, we must also stand against other things. Paul said, "Having done all to stand, stand therefore" (Eph. 6:13-14). This was a Greek military phrase in Paul's time that alluded to being in a heated battle and becoming weak, but girding up your armor and continuing to fight until you are standing in victory.

Christ warned His followers of the dangers of offenses, betrayals, and love growing cold at the time of the end. He made this powerful statement: "But he that endures to the end shall be saved" (Matt. 24:10-13). People have left churches over offense, disagreement, bitterness, or other carnal reasons, and are no longer standing strong. They refuse to attend church, never realizing they are being weakened by lack of fellowship in God's presence.

The Greek word endure means *to stand firm, persevere, to bear up under.* It can be the image of a soldier going into battle, carrying the weight of his weapons, shield, and other equipment. He must bear up under and endure hardness as a good soldier of Jesus Christ (2 Tim. 2:3). This Greek word *hardness* alludes to *suffering together with others for the same cause,* or *to partner in afflictions.*

The point is that we are not to be alone in this endurance test, or in these final conflicts where light and darkness are clashing. At times, we need others to stand with us and help us bear up under the load. Even Christ, in a time of suffering, needed help carrying the cross to His final destination (Matt. 27:32). When you are weak, keep standing. If you fall, get back up.

4. Be on Guard for the Tempter

While Christ prayed in the Garden of Gethsemane, His eleven disciples, including his inner circle, Peter, James and John, slept. Christ awakened them, but a short time later, their eyelids were again closed. They were out cold, lying between olive trees and rocks.

Jesus knew that within a few hours, Peter would face his most severe test since being chosen as a disciple. He would slice off the ear of the servant of the high priest, then sit by a fire and place a curse, called an anathema, upon himself. He went from fishing on a sailboat to being sifted in the proverbial frying pan.

After the first hour of intense prayer, when Christ found them sleeping, He spoke these words directly to Peter: "Could you not watch with me one hour?" Notice He did not ask, "Could you not pray?" Instead, He was asking them to stay awake and be alert.

Christ then told them, "Watch and pray, that you enter not into temptation. The spirit is indeed willing, but the flesh is weak" (Matt. 26:41). The spirit is your spiritual center. The flesh is the carnal force that drives you away from God and toward sin. The spirit tells us to fast, and the flesh says it's time to eat. The spirit says pray, while the flesh wants to sleep. If you can't fall asleep at night, start praying and I can almost guarantee that you will fall asleep.

Most temptation that pulls on the flesh occurs when you are alone with time to think, or when you are with friends who pressure you to do something counter to your convictions, something that pierces your conscience. This is the reason we are to watch—stay sober, alert and on guard—and pray. A combination of both is necessary. Temptation comes in cycles and seasons. Be on guard and know that seasons and cycles will come and go; if you stay alert, you can resist the tempter.

5. Underrated Blessing and Overrated Fears

The most powerful emotion in the world, in my opinion, is fear. I have been told that when a person loses their temper, it raises blood pressure, and the intense anger weakens the immune system for up to eight hours. The same is true with fear. When the virus began taking the lives of so many Christians, fear gripped believers who were diagnosed with the virus. My wife experienced a bad case of the virus and was taken by an ambulance to the emergency room. She was hospitalized and treated for five days.

To defeat fear, she listened to praise and worship songs for twelve hours a day. She refused to listen to negative news or to people on television talking about Covid deaths. She did not turn the television on in her room the entire time. She wanted faith and God's presence to overcome any fear.

On one occasion, the disciples saw a miracle where a boy's lunch of two fish and five loaves of bread was blessed by Christ and multiplied into a meal that fed five-thousand men. Twelve baskets were left over for the boy, who received a good return on his investment.

After this miracle, the disciples were instructed to get into a boat and go over to the other side of the lake. On the way, a storm with contrary winds hit, frightening the boatload of fearful followers. Jesus came walking on the water, where He entered the boat and calmed them down. How could they see such a stunning miracle, then just a few hours later, fall into a pit of unbelief? Mark wrote, "For they considered not the miracle of the loaves, for their hearts were hardened" (Mark 6:52).

We underrate God's blessings and overrate our fears. To maintain a strong faith each day, it is important to recall *faith memories*; or as David did, to recall the great events God did in the past, and believe that God will repeat them in the future. In the time of the end, men's hearts will fail them for fear, and for looking after those things which are coming on the earth (Luke 21:26). This Greek word *fear* is *phobos*, from which we get *phobia*, meaning irrational or excessive fear of a thing or a situation, which might create dread or panic. Among the Greeks, Phobos was a god responsible for creating fear during the time of war. The Romans, in their mythology, referred to him as Pavor, also called Terror. Consider how the purpose of terrorism is to create fear and panic among people. The Bible calls fear a (demonic) spirit and teaches that "God has not given us a spirit of fear, but of power and of love and of a sound mind" (2 Tim. 1:7).

We underrate God's ability when we forget all He has done for us—answered prayers, strength, joy, health, peace, and healing. Fear will prevail when faith is absent. It is impossible to overrate God, as all things are possible with Him (Mark 10:27).

6. Never Lose Your Hope

Abraham knew that he was an old man and Sarah was barren, yet we read, "[Abraham] who against hope believed in hope, that he might become the father of many nations" (Rom. 4:18). Faith and hope are God's power twins. In the Greek New Testament, the word hope alludes to an earnest expectation and an attitude of confidently waiting and looking forward. *Faith believes for it, but hope waits for it.*

Why is hope so important? When you lose faith, it becomes impossible to please God and your blessings can be put on hold. When you choose to give up faith and hope, you release your legal right to be under God's hedge and favor. Giving up would be like pleading guilty before the trial begins. What you say is used against you in court, and the same is true in the courtroom of heaven.

This is why hope deferred (or delayed) makes the heart sick (Prov. 13:12). Doctors have told me that hope is one of the most powerful forces that keeps sick people alive and extends their days. Once a person loses hope, it seems their mind, body, and spirit begin to shut down.

7. Discover the Power of Communion

The word communion is used here to refer to the Lord's Supper, or the Eucharist, which consists of the sacred bread and the fruit of the vine. On the eve of Passover, Christ introduced the New Covenant through His body (the bread) and His blood (the fruit of the vine). The first imagery of the bread and wine is found in Genesis 14:18 when the first king-priest, Melchizedek, offered the bread and wine to Abraham as a sign of covenant.

The Israelites were slaves in Egypt. On the night before their mass exodus from Egypt, the angel of death passed throughout the whole land, taking with him the firstborn from every Egyptian home. The only exemption from this appointment with death occurred at the houses of the Hebrews, where the lamb's blood was visible on the right, top, and center of the exterior doorpost. That night, the Hebrew families joined together to eat the lamb under the blood covering.

From this powerful narrative, I preached a message called *Plagues, Pestilences, and the Power of Communion*. When we partake of the Lord's Supper in faith and understand that His blood has redeemed us from sin and His body was bruised for our healing, we can lay claim to our own spiritual, emotional, and physical healing.

Full Gospel and Evangelical congregations must renew an emphasis on the understanding of the Lord's Supper, and the power of this covenant service.

8. Do Your First Works When Necessary

In Revelation, Christ instructed the church at Ephesus to repent and do their first works (Rev. 2:5). The believer's first works allude to the foundational level of works or action. Repentance and water baptism combined are our first works. The first command for those in sin is to repent and be baptized (Acts 2:38). There are times when we fall short or struggle with unforgiveness and other sins of the flesh and spirit. Scripture requires us to cleanse ourselves (2 Cor. 7:1).

At a Summer Ramp conference in Hamilton, Alabama, I was assisting in baptizing hundreds of young people in Williams Creek on property owned by Karen Wheaton, founder of Ramp Ministries. Toward the conclusion, I heard the Holy Spirit tell me, "Do your first works again and be re-baptized." I felt in my spirit that if I obeyed this instruction, then offense, wounds, and repressed anger I had been carrying would be washed away through water baptism.

At the conclusion, I asked one of the Ramp ministers to re-baptize me. When I came up, every part of my heart and spirit felt completely clean and released. I honestly was stunned at the instant peace I experienced. Since that time, I have encouraged men and women who have battled negative emotions and wounded hearts to release the person or people involved back to God for Him to deal with. It is up to God to determine who He will judge and what words and actions people will answer for at the heavenly judgment.

It is imperative in these last days to keep your spirit clean, your mind clear, and your heart pure. By doing so, the adversary has nothing in you that he can hold on to.

9. Loose Yourself from Financial Pressure

I understand financial pressure. For years, I felt financial responsibility for four large buildings, the salaries of forty-five workers, utility bills, grounds maintenance, insurance, and everything else that comes with running ministries. After hearing from the Lord, I began to release myself from certain ministry responsibilities by handing them over for others to direct. I also focused on other forms of media outreach and cut back on some television stations, saving substantial amounts of revenue. This lifted a financial burden that I had carried for many years.

Financial pressure and the weight of carrying that kind of burden creates cares of ministry or cares of life. The pressure of dealing with this will slowly choke the peace and joy from you.

There are ways to release yourself from financial burdens. These include paying off all credit card debt, selling things you do not need, not buying anything you don't need and cannot afford, and finding common sense ways to cut down on expenses in every area possible.

10. Find a Strong Prayer Group

One of the great outreaches we have in Cleveland, Tennessee is our weekly Thursday night world prayer, which has continued non-stop for over ten years. It is refreshing, encouraging, and exciting to join with over a hundred intercessors and pray for an hour of livestreamed prayer, because we know our prayers are being heard and will also be answered.

I want to make a strong statement that I believe one hundred percent. If you do not learn how to live a life of prayer, spend quality time with the Lord, and listen to the Holy Spirit, you will not maintain the strength and endurance you need to stand in the evil day.

If you do not have a prayer group, please join our team, either at the ISOW building or online at 6 PM (EST) on Thursday evenings for one hour of live prayer.

CHAPTER 24

FINDING A SAFE HAVEN AT THE TIME OF THE END

Sometime in the future, a set time that the Bible calls *the trib-ulation* (Matt. 24:29) or *great tribulation* (Matt. 24:21) will be unleashed on earth. When this season arrives, a prophetic clock will be set in the heavens; and seven years later, Christ will return to Jerusalem (Zech. 14:4).

This global season of trouble is divided into two distinct halves, each continuing for forty-two months (Rev. 11:2; 13:5). When the set time of the final tribulation arrives, Daniel noted, "…there shall be a time of trouble, such as never was since there was a nation even to that same time …" (Dan. 12:1). Christ said, "For then shall be great tribu-lation, such as was not since the beginning of the world to this time, no, nor ever shall be" (Matt. 24:21). Christ also noted, "Except those days (of the tribulation) should be shortened, there should no flesh be saved" (Matt. 24:22).

There are three reasons why the 2,520 days of this global crisis will be the worst time ever recorded in world history. First, the Antichrist will fight numerous wars. After he gains the influence and respect of ten kings ruling ten nations, the armies from each nation will unite and form a massive military coalition to assist the Antichrist in going forth "conquering and to conquer" (Rev. 6:2). Daniel warned of this final dictator, saying that "by peace he shall destroy many" (Dan. 8:25).

The Apostle John notes in Revelation 13:4 that the world will ask this question when the Antichrist seizes global control: "Who is like the beast? Who is able to make war with him?" In Revelation chapter 6, when the four spirit horsemen are released, two of the four riders carry a great sword, a symbol that alludes to death, fighting, and war (Rev. 6:4, 8). When the horsemen ride, John writes that peace is taken from the earth. The combined death toll from seven years of tribulation is unknown, but we can assume it will be in the hundreds of millions, and possibly billions.

The second reason the tribulation will historically be like no other time is due to a severe famine that leads to hyperinflation, where scholars have noted that one loaf of bread will cost a day's wages (Rev. 6:6). One fourth of the earth's population will face death by the sword (war and fighting) and by hunger, pestilence, and beasts of the field (Rev. 6:8). If the world's population at the time is eight billion, this means that two billion people will die from these means alone.

When the ancient city of Jerusalem was under siege, Roman soldiers blocked access into or out of the city. A severe famine followed, and after months of isolation, people were starving. In Judea, some were boiling their boots and eating the leather, while others were eating bits of straw they found in animal stalls in the city. According to Josephus, one mother killed and boiled her own infant child to have something to eat. History shows that when people move from *hunger* to *starvation*, they lose all moral restraint. They will rob, steal, and even kill other people to feed themselves and their families.

A third reason the tribulation will be the most severe humanitarian and ecological crisis on record is the sheer number of natural disasters (trumpet and bowl judgments in Revelation) that will impact every nation on the planet. One cosmic disaster will be an asteroid strike that will pollute the drinking water and rivers, and make a third of the waters bitter and poisonous. Many will die from the water. Around the same time, a mountain burning with fire (likely a massive volcanic eruption) will collapse into the sea and create a tsunami that destroys a third of the sea life and the ships (Rev. 8:7-9). Another historic natural calamity is recorded in Revelation 16:18-20, where a mega earthquake will cause the cities of the nations to fall and every island and mountain to disappear. John wrote that this will be a great earthquake such as was not since men were upon the earth (Rev. 16:18). These combined natural calamities alone will cause untold damage, along with an astronomical number of deaths.

SOME PEOPLE WILL SURVIVE

As impossible as it may seem, at the conclusion of the seven years, there will be people who have survived these horrible calamities. They will be living when Christ returns with the armies of heaven (Rev. 19:11-21). Christ taught that when He returns, "All of the tribes of the earth shall mourn, and they shall see the Son of man coming in the clouds of heaven with power and great glory" (Matt. 24:30). The Lord further reveals: "And he shall send his angels with a great sound of a trumpet, and they shall gather together his elect from the four winds, from one end of heaven to the other" (Matt. 24:31).

Scripture gives no indication of the places or nations where people will endure and survive the great tribulation. In the Apocalypse, John gave percentages, telling us that over one-third of the earth and one-fourth of the population will suffer from certain destructive impacts. John noted that when the predicted natural disasters begin, men will run to the mountains, dens, and caves, hiding themselves to avoid death and destruction. Those fleeing include kings, great men, rich men, captains, common men, and slaves (Rev. 6:15). These dens could include large government bunkers and underground military bases that have been constructed in modern times in case of nuclear disaster.

Many people will receive Christ during the tribulation, then be martyred by the Antichrist and his henchmen. These will die by beheading for refusing to take the mark of the beast and worship his image. These martyrs will be resurrected at the conclusion of the seven-year tribulation, and they will live and reign with Christ for a thousand years (Rev. 20:4). When Christ rules and reigns in Jerusalem for a thousand years, the earth will be repopulated by those who survived the tribulation. Satan and all demonic spirits will be bound and confined in the abyss (Rev. 20:1-2).

A review of future events creates an image of doom and gloom. This perception causes some to reject or refuse to read the biblical warnings of what is to come. Ignoring the facts may temporarily ease your mind, but that will not prevent the prophecies from being fulfilled. Three spiritual truths will encourage Christian when they study the Bible's apocalyptic warnings.

SATAN'S TIME IS LIMITED

First, as biblical prophecies continue to be fulfilled, Satan knows that his time is short. John wrote that Satan will be expelled from the second heaven to earth during the final forty-two months of the tribulation. John says that, at this point, Satan will know he is running out of time. Thus, our adversary's time is limited.

Believers, however, *are not running out of time.* We have been imparted with eternal life through Christ, and our destiny includes ruling with Him for a thousand years. Afterward, all saints will live for eternity on a new earth and in the New Jerusalem, which will come down to earth from heaven (Rev. 21 and 22). Forty-two months is less than one term of a United States president. God allows presidents more time to serve America than He will allow Satan to control the nations on earth.

THE TRIBULATION HAS AN EXPIRATION DATE

The second truth is that the tribulation is a set season that has an *expiration date*. Personally, I believe the tribulation will begin near the same time as the *catching away* of the overcoming saints (1 Thess. 4:16-17), then continue for a pre-determined time.

As previously stated, the actual rule of the Antichrist begins in the *middle* of a final seven-year timeframe (Dan. 9:27). When Satan is cast down to the earth (Rev. 12:7-9), he will supernaturally empower the Antichrist, giving him his power, seat (throne), and authority (Rev. 13:2). Here again, the time period is preset for forty-two months (Rev. 13:5). The tribulation, the power of Satan, and the rule of the Antichrist is limited. None on earth or in heaven can add to or take away from God's plan.

THE EARTH WILL BE RESTORED

The third important biblical fact is that, despite the massive damage to the world's cities, the wars, the destruction of global food supplies, the burning of trees and grass, the pollution of waters, and so on, the earth will eventually *fully recover* under a special blessing of restoration through Christ's political, economic, and spiritual leadership. He will rule the nations "with a rod of iron," a metaphor alluding to Christ's complete control over the kings of the world (Rev. 12:5). His iron rule will be comparable to a shepherd who uses an iron stick to protect his flocks from dangerous animals.

Old Testament prophets, at times, peered past a dark veil into the future and gave us a preview of the Messiah's reign on earth. Ezekiel detailed the temple that will be erected in Jerusalem, where Christ will sit upon His throne and receive gifts and worship from all ethnic groups from Gentile nations (Ezekiel 44-47).

The global restoration will be similar to how the world recovered and was repopulated after the massive flood of Noah's day. Once the flood waters receded, grass reappeared, trees regrew and produced fruit, animals reproduced, and the earth blossomed again. I call this the second creation, with the Garden of Eden being the first. Life was restored, cities were built, nations were established, and human dwellings were erected in the plains of Shinar (Gen. 11).

WE ARE NOT THERE YET

Despite global shutdowns, economic crisis, shortages, wars, crime, plague, and division, the world presently is in the season of the birth pangs of the Messiah—the beginning of sorrows (Matt. 24:8). Birth pangs will include famines, pestilences, earthquakes (and other natural disasters, such as droughts, tsunamis, floods, hurricanes, and tornados), wars, and rumors of wars. We will see occurrences that impact daily lives. Just as a woman's birth pangs intensify the closer to the child's birth, cosmic and earthly disasters will increase in duration and frequency.

Christ warned that in this world we will have tribulation, meaning trouble, distress, persecution, mental pressure, and anxiety (John 16:33). However, based upon numerous prophecies that reveal things that transpire before and during the early stages of the great tribulation, I do not believe we have yet entered the tribulation as spoken of in the book of Revelation. We are, however, experiencing previews of events to come.

The times and seasons the world is experiencing remind me of the gap that existed a few years before the Roman Tenth Legion destroyed

Jerusalem. When Emperor Nero died (June 9, AD 68), there was a transition in emperors. Vespasian, who initiated the assault against Jewish rebels in Judea and Jerusalem, was elected Emperor in Rome, which opened the door for his son Titus to oversee his father's former military activities. Eventually, he directed the final siege of Jerusalem and the destruction of the temple on the ninth of Av in the year AD 70.

From AD 66 to AD 70, there was a brief opening in Jerusalem in which both Jews and Christians could make a life-or-death decision to either get out of Jerusalem and Judea or remain in the city. If they stayed, they could join the rebels in hopes of experiencing divine intervention that would empower the Jews to defeat the Roman legions and rescue the city from destruction. Most Christians dwelling in Jerusalem and Judea remembered Christ's warning: when you see foreign armies preparing to surround the city, flee to the mountains (Matt. 24:16).

A large population of Christians met together to decide what they should do. After prayer and the reading of Christ's prophetic warnings, along with a warning that an early church father stated was from an angel, they decided they should leave. They packed up, left their lands and homes, and resettled across the Jordan River in a Gentile city called Pella. A generation earlier, the ministry of Christ and the apostles had made a dramatic impact on the region, as many accepted the Christian message and the miracles that followed. The citizens of Pella welcomed the Judean Christians with open arms. For many years, Christians built a strong faith community in the region. The decision to leave the city and transition to a new location proved to be a correct one.

LESSONS FROM JERUSALEM'S CHRISTIANS

Presently, thousands of people are moving from America's large cities to other states or smaller communities. In the future, due to insecurity and danger, there will be few safe havens throughout the world, especially in large population centers. However, at this present time, there are communities and smaller cities that offer a bit more security, freedom, and faith than other areas. It has become obvious that, within the United States, there are clear-cut moral, spiritual, and political divisions between the people and even cities and states.

Divisions in the United States have created opposing sides that are as different as oil and water. We have believers versus unbelievers. We have those who want freedom and the opportunity to pursue life without tyranny, versus radical leftists with socialist, Marxist, or communist agendas. There are flag wavers and flag burners, Bible lovers and Bible haters, morality seekers and promoters of abominations, lovers of truth and lovers of lies. America's division and the political, moral, and spiritual climate of our nation has opened an abyss so large that, without divine intervention and spiritual revival and restoration, no bridge can unite these divided states of America. Polls seem to indicate that our population is stuck at a 50-50 split—the same percentages that seem to emerge during every presidential election.

America's secular, leftist media have become a cadre of psychobabblers, legends in their own minds, and political puppets of propaganda, working with their masters who pull their strings. An evil agenda that once was intentionally concealed is now openly flaunted, almost like a religion of its own, with worshippers in a trance as they absorb and repeat the propaganda of the talking heads. Lies are truth and facts are whatever you report them to be. Freedom is on the chopping block.

When the Roman legions were setting their faces and pointing their swords toward the ancient Holy Land, bold men who were willing to die free instead of live as Roman slaves seized control of the mountain strongholds of Gamala in the Golan Heights and Masada in the southern Judean Wilderness. Many Jews left the city of Jerusalem to live with their families in more secluded parts of the country.

Eventually, Gamala, Masada, and Jerusalem fell to the Romans, as the Roman leaders were intent on stopping any rebellion against Rome. In AD 67, men in Gamala jumped from the clifftops to avoid being captured. In Masada, 960 Jews either killed each other or committed suicide to avoid being captured or killed by Roman troops. For these ancient people, dying free was better than living in chains.

Right now in the United States, people are fleeing some states, especially the West Coast, and moving to Midwestern or Southeastern states. I personally have met many from California. The extremely high taxes and cost of living, the radical ideology and political leadership, and the anti-Christian attitude from many civil and state leaders have combined to force an exodus from certain states. When I have asked those from the West Coast or other states why they left and moved to our area in Tennessee, here is a summary of their answers:

- The tax rates were astronomical, and the state of Tennessee levies no state tax on personal income. (The tax rates in many southern states are much lower than West Coast and Northeastern states.)

- We were able to sell our home and buy a home in the East with land for half the cost.

- Schools where we came from are teaching things that are contrary to the moral and biblical principles that we want our children to follow.

- The cities are becoming more dangerous, and mob violence is more common than in the East.

- There is an all-out assault on Christian values in the state we left.

- The state was attacking our Constitutional rights.

The days of Noah are an example of global judgment (by water), whereas the biblical account of Lot reveals the act of *selective* judgment. In Noah's time, all cities and towns were under water. In Lot's time, out of five cities, four were burned to ashes. However, one small town named Zoar remained safe. It was built on a high mountain, a safe distance from the fire and brimstone exploding in the valley. One location was safe, while the others were burning in the danger zone.

In the United States are cities that were unknowingly built on major earthquake fault lines. The East Coast can suffer deadly and damaging hurricanes. Tornadoes strike the flatlands in the Midwest. Floods can strike anywhere. Disasters can damage vehicles, homes, businesses, and land. But your most important asset is your family: your companion, children, grandchildren and close relatives.

FOCUSING ON YOUR NEEDS

Humans want their needs and desires to be fulfilled. Our basic human needs are food, water, shelter, clothing, and safety. Americans are career oriented, though. Many earned a four-year college degree or higher, hoping the additional academic education would increase their employment value. The American dream includes a good job or career that allows you to make, save, and invest money; a home of your own, maybe with some land; a family and children; a secure retirement; and the ability to settle down at retirement to enjoy the autumn years.

Often when I'm stuck in traffic in Atlanta or another major city, I'm reminded that no job and no amount of income is worth spending hours every day, morning and evening, in a long line of metal and rubber, getting home even later when any kind of accident blocks the highways. For others, the weekly paycheck is worth the daily disruptions.

Knowing the will of God for you and your family is the key. In the time of Babylonian captivity, tens of thousands of Jews were forced to march in servitude to Babylon for seventy years. However, the prophet Jeremiah and a small remnant of Jews were allowed to remain. Jeremiah was permitted to live in Mizpah under the watchful eye of the governor. According to church tradition and extra-biblical sources, he was later brought into Egypt by a group of Jewish rebels.

Believers are salt and light in a corrupt world (Matt. 5:13-14). For some, the will of God is to remain where you are as a witness, to reflect God's love in a dark world. For others, perhaps those in a future judgment zone, a door may open for you to transition to another location. Many older Americans are choosing to live in smaller communities where people know and watch out for their neighbors and where they can be involved in activities and worship in a local church.

People shouldn't haphazardly make a knee-jerk move without prayer and wise decision making. Are jobs or business opportunities available in the new location? Can you find an affordable place to live? What is the long-term benefit of a permanent move? It is not wisdom just to pack up your car without a plan of action or knowing God's will in the situation.

YOUR GREATEST SECURITY

A Christian's greatest security is to abide in the secret place under the shadow of the Almighty (Psalm 91). This requires maintaining a daily pray life, reading the Bible, and keeping your faith and trust in the Almighty. Believers must remember that we have advocates. One is Christ, who represents us in heaven, and the other is the Holy Spirit, who is with us on earth. Christ oversees our needs of redemption and our prayers, while the Holy Spirit oversees our personal situations on earth (John 14:14-17; 1 John 2:1). The Holy Spirit is assigned to warn us of coming trouble, as seen throughout the ministry of Christ and the book of Acts. He is able to show us things to come (John 16:13).

It was a challenge for prophets in the Bible to warn the political and spiritual leaders of danger coming, as the warnings were often mocked. In the case of Jeremiah's warning of the Babylonian invasion, the warning took forty years to fulfill. With the visions I have shared that have not come to pass, I suggest we heed the words of Christ to watch and pray (Matt. 26:41); the admonition of Paul, to pray without ceasing (1 Thess. 5:17); and the instruction of Jude, to build ourselves up in the faith by praying in the Holy Spirit (Jude 20).